Shekspear's

Tucker Brooke

Copyright © BiblioLife, LLC

This book represents a historical reproduction of a work originally published before 1923 that is part of a unique project which provides opportunities for readers, educators and researchers by bringing hard-to-find original publications back into print at reasonable prices. Because this and other works are culturally important, we have made them available as part of our commitment to protecting, preserving and promoting the world's literature. These books are in the "public domain" and were digitized and made available in cooperation with libraries, archives, and open source initiatives around the world dedicated to this important mission.

We believe that when we undertake the difficult task of re-creating these works as attractive, readable and affordable books, we further the goal of sharing these works with a global audience, and preserving a vanishing wealth of human knowledge.

Many historical books were originally published in small fonts, which can make them very difficult to read. Accordingly, in order to improve the reading experience of these books, we have created "enlarged print" versions of our books. Because of font size variation in the original books, some of these may not technically qualify as "large print" books, as that term is generally defined; however, we believe these versions provide an overall improved reading experience for many.

SHAKESPEARE'S PLUTARCH : EDITED BY C. F. TUCKER BROOKE
B.Litt. : Vol. I. : CONTAINING THE MAIN SOURCES OF JULIUS CAESAR

CHATTO & WINDUS, PUBLISHERS
LONDON MCMIX

All rights reserved

SHAKESPEARE'S PLUTARCH

This Special Edition of 'SHAKESPEARE'S PLUTARCH' *is limited to* 1000 *copies, of which* 500 *are reserved for America.*

THE LIVES
OF THE NOBLE GRE-
CIANS AND ROMANES, COMPARED
together by that graue learned *Philosopher* and *Historiographer*, *Plutarke of Chæronea*:

Translated out of Greeke into French by IAMES AMYOT, Abbot of Bellozane,
Bishop of Auxerre, one of the Kings priuy counsel, and great Amner
of Fraunce, and out of French into Englishe, by
Thomas North.

Imprinted at London by Thomas Vautroullier
and Iohn VVight.
1579.

THE LIFE OF JULIUS CAESAR

AT what time Sylla was made Lord of all, he would have had Caesar put away his wife Cornelia, the daughter of Cinna Dictator: but, when he saw he could neither with any promise nor threat bring him to it, he took her jointure away from him. The cause of Caesar's ill-will unto Sylla was by means of marriage: for Marius th' elder married his father's own sister, by whom he had Marius the younger, whereby Caesar and he were cousin germans. Sylla being troubled in weighty matters, putting to death so many of his enemies, when he came to be conqueror, he made no reckoning of Caesar: but he was not contented to be hidden in safety, but came and made suit unto the people for the Priesthoodship that was void, when he had scant any hair on his face. Howbeit he was repulsed by Sylla's means, that secretly was against him. Who when he was determined to have killed him, some of his friends told him that it was to no purpose to put so young a boy as he to death. But Sylla told them again, that they did not consider that there were many Marians in that young boy. Caesar, understanding that, stale out of Rome, and hid

Caesar joined with Cinna and Marius

himself a long time in the country of the Sabines, wandering still from place to place. But one day, being carried from house to house, he fell into the hands of Sylla's soldiers, who searched all those places, and took them whom they found hidden. Caesar bribed the captain, whose name was Cornelius, with two talents which he gave him. After he had escaped them thus, he went unto the seaside and took ship, and sailed into Bithynia to go unto King Nicomedes. When he had been with him a while, he took sea again, and was taken by pirates about the Isle of Pharmacusa: for those pirates kept all upon that sea-coast, with a great fleet of ships and boats. They asking him at the first twenty talents for his ransom, Caesar laughed them to scorn, as though they knew not what a man they had taken, and of himself promised them fifty talents. Then he sent his men up and down to get him this money, so that he was left in manner alone among these thieves of the Cilicians (which are the cruellest butchers in the world), with one of his friends, and two of his slaves only: and yet he made so little reckoning of them, that, when he was desirous to sleep, he sent unto them to command them to make no noise. Thus was he eight-and-thirty days among them, not kept as prisoner, but rather waited upon by them as a prince. All this time he would boldly exercise himself in any sport or pastime they would go to. And other while also he would write verses, and make

Caesar took sea and went unto Nicomedes, king of Bithynia.

Caesar taken of pirates.

orations, and call them together to say them before them : and if any of them seemed as though they had not understood him, or passed not for them, he called them blockheads and brute beasts, and, laughing, threatened them that he would hang them up. But they were as merry with the matter as could be, and took all in good part, thinking that this his bold speech came through the simplicity of his youth. So, when his ransom was come from the city of Miletus, they being paid their money, and he again set at liberty, he then presently armed, and manned out certain ships out of the haven of Miletus, to follow those thieves, whom he found yet riding at anchor in the same island. So he took the most of them, and had the spoil of their goods, but for their bodies, he brought them into the city of Pergamum, and there committed them to prison, whilst he himself went to speak with Junius, who had the government of Asia, as unto whom the execution of these pirates did belong, for that he was Praetor of that country. *Junius praetor of Asia.* But this Praetor, having a great fancy to be fingering of the money, because there was good store of it, answered, that he would consider of these prisoners at better leisure. Caesar, leaving Junius there, returned again unto Pergamum, and there hung up all these thieves openly upon a cross, as he had oftentimes promised them in the isle he would do, when they thought he did but jest. Afterwards, when Sylla's power began to decay, Caesar's friends wrote unto him, to pray him to come home again. But he sailed first unto Rhodes, to study there a time under Apollonius the son of Molon, whose scholar also Cicero was, for he was a very honest man, and an excellent good rhetorician. It is reported that Caesar had an excellent natural gift to speak well before the people, and, besides that rare gift, he was excellently well studied, so that doubtless he was counted the second man for eloquence in his time, and gave place to the first because he would be the first and chiefest man of war and authority, being not yet come to the degree of perfection to speak well, which his nature could have performed in him, because he was given rather to follow wars and to manage great matters, which in th' end brought him to be Lord of all Rome. And therefore, in a book he wrote against that which Cicero made in the praise of Cato, he prayeth the readers not to compare the style of a soldier with the eloquence of an excellent orator, that had followed it the most part of his life. When he was returned again unto Rome, he accused Dolabella for his ill-behaviour in the government of his province, and he had divers cities of Greece that gave in evidence against him. Notwithstanding, Dolabella at the length was dismissed. Caesar, to requite the goodwill of the Grecians, which they had shewed him in his accusation of Dolabella, took their cause in hand, when they did accuse Publius Antonius before Marcus Lucullus, Praetor of Macedon: and followed it so hard against him in their behalf, that Antonius was driven to

JULIUS CAESAR

appeal before the Tribunes at Rome, alleging, to colour his appeal withal, that he could have no justice in Greece against the Grecians. Now Caesar immediately wan many men's goodwills at Rome, through his eloquence in pleading of their causes: and the people loved him marvellously also, because of the courteous manner he had to speak to every man, and to use them gently, being more ceremonious therein than was looked for in one of his years. Furthermore, he ever kept a good board, and fared well at his table, and was very liberal besides: the which indeed did advance him forward, and brought him in estimation with the people. His enemies, judging that this favour of the common people would soon quail, when he could no longer hold out that charge and expense, suffered him to run on, till by little and little he was grown to be of great strength and power. But in fine, when they had thus given him the bridle to grow to this greatness, and that they could not then pull him back, though indeed in sight it would turn one day to the destruction of the whole state and commonwealth of Rome: too late they found, that there is not so little a beginning of anything, but continuance of time will soon make it strong, when through contempt there is no impediment to hinder the greatness. Thereupon Cicero, like a wise shipmaster that feareth the calmness of the sea, was the first man that, mistrusting his manner of dealing in the commonwealth, found out his

Caesar loved hospitality.

Caesar a follower of the people.

JULIUS CAESAR

craft and malice, which he cunningly cloked under the habit of outward courtesy and familiarity. 'And yet,' said he, 'when I consider how finely he combeth his fair bush of hair, and how smooth it lieth, and that I see him scratch his head with one finger only: my mind gives me then that such a kind of man should not have so wicked a thought in his head, as to overthrow the state of the commonwealth.' But this was long time after that. The first show and proof of the love and good will which the people did bear unto Caesar was when he sued to be Tribune of the soldiers (to wit, Colonel of a thousand footmen), standing against Caius Pompilius, at what time he was preferred and chosen before him. But the second, and more manifest proof than the first, was at the death of his aunt Julia, the wife of Marius the elder. For, being her nephew, he made a solemn oration in the market-place in commendation of her, and at her burial did boldly venture to show forth the images of Marius: the which was the first time that they were seen after Sylla's victory, because that Marius and all his confederates had been proclaimed traitors and enemies to the commonwealth. For, when there were some that cried out upon Caesar for doing of it, the people on th' other side kept a stir, and rejoiced at it, clapping of their hands, and thanked him for that he had brought as it were out of hell the remembrance of Marius' honour

JULIUS CAESAR

again unto Rome, which had so long time been obscured
and buried. And where it had been an ancient
custom of long time that the Romans used to make
funeral orations in praise of old ladies and matrons
when they died, but not of young women, Caesar
was the first that praised his own wife with funeral oration
when she was dead, the which also did increase the people's
good wills the more, seeing him of so kind and gentle
nature. After the burial of his wife he was made
Treasurer under Antistius Vetus Praetor, whom he
honoured ever after: so that when himself came
to be Praetor, he made his son to be chosen Treasurer.
Afterwards, when he was come out of that office,
he married his third wife Pompeia, having a
daughter by his first wife Cornelia, which was
married unto Pompey the Great. Now for that he was
very liberal in expenses, buying (as some thought) but a
vain and short glory of the favour of the people (where
indeed he bought good cheap the greatest things that could
be), some say that, before he bare any office in the commonwealth, he was grown in debt to the sum of thirteen
hundred talents. Furthermore, because he was made overseer of the work for the highway going unto Appius, he
disbursed a great sum of his own money towards the charges
of the same. And on the other side, when he was made
Aedilis, for that he did show the people the pastime of
three hundred and twenty couple of sword players, and did

Caesar the first that praised his wife in funeral oration.

Caesar made Quaestor.

Pompeia, Caesar's third wife.

besides exceed all other in sumptuousness in the sports
and common feasts which he made to delight them
withal, (and did as it were drown all the stately
shows of others in the like, that had gone before
him), he so pleased the people, and wan their love therewith, that they devised daily to give him new offices for to
requite him. At that time there were two factions
in Rome, to wit, the faction of Sylla, which was very strong
and of great power, and the other of Marius, which then
was under foot and durst not shew itself. But Caesar,
because he would renew it again, even at that time when,
he being Aedilis, all the feasts and common sports were in
their greatest ruff, he secretly caused images of Marius to
be made, and of victories that carried triumphs, and those
he set up one night within the Capitol. The next morning,
when every man saw the glistering of these golden images
excellently well wrought, shewing by the inscriptions that
they were the victories which Marius had won upon the
Cimbrians, every one marvelled much at the boldness of
him that durst set them up there, knowing well enough who
it was. Hereupon it ran straight through all the city, and
every man came thither to see them. Then some cried out
upon Caesar, and said it was a tyranny which he
meant to set up, by renewing of such honours
as before had been trodden under foot, and forgotten, by common decree and open proclamation:
and that it was no more but a bait to gauge the people's

Caesar's prodigality.

Caesar accused to make a rebellion in the state.

JULIUS CAESAR

good wills, which he had set out in the stately shews of his common plays, to see if he had brought them to his lure, that they would abide such parts to be played, and a new alteration of things to be made. They of Marius' faction on th' other side, encouraging one another, shewed themselves straight a great number gathered together, and made the mount of the Capitol ring again with their cries and clapping of hands: insomuch as the tears ran down many of their cheeks for very joy, when they saw the images of Marius, and they extolled Caesar to the skies, judging him the worthiest man of all the kindred of Marius. The Senate being assembled thereupon, Catulus Luctatius, one of the greatest authority at that time in Rome, rose, and vehemently inveighed against Caesar, and spake that then which ever since hath been noted much: that Caesar did not now covertly go to work, but by plain force sought to alter the state of the commonwealth. Nevertheless, Caesar at that time answered him so that the Senate was satisfied. Thereupon they that had him in estimation did grow in better hope than before, and persuaded him, that hardily he should give place to no man, and that through the good will of the people he should be better than all they, and come to be the chiefest man of the city. At that time the chief Bishop Metellus died, and two of the notablest men of the city, and of greatest authority, (Isauricus and Catulus), contended for his room: Caesar, notwithstanding their contention, would *The death of Metellus, chief Bishop of Rome* give neither of them both place, but presented himself to the people, and made suit for it as they did. The suit being equal betwixt either of them, Catulus, because he was a man of greater calling and dignity than the other, doubting the uncertainty of the election, sent unto Caesar a good sum of money, to make him leave off his suit. But Caesar sent him word again, that he would lend a greater sum than that, to maintain the suit against him. When the day of th' election came, his mother bringing him to the door of his house, Caesar, weeping, kissed her, and said: 'Mother, this day thou shalt see thy son chief Bishop of Rome, or banished from Rome.' In fine, when the voices of the people were gathered together, and the strife well debated, Caesar wan the victory, and made the Senate and noblemen all afraid of him, for that they thought that thenceforth he would make the people do what he thought good. Then Catulus and Piso fell flatly out with Cicero, and condemned him for that he did not bewray Caesar, when he knew that he was of conspiracy with Catiline, and had opportunity to have done it. For when Catiline was bent and determined, not only to overthrow the state of the commonwealth, but utterly to destroy the empire of Rome, he scaped out of the hands of justice for lack of sufficient proof, before his full treason and determination was known. Notwithstanding he left Lentulus and Cethegus in the city, companions of his

Caesar made chief Bishop of Rome.

Caesar suspected to be confederate with Catiline in his conspiracy.

JULIUS CAESAR

conspiracy: unto whom whether Caesar did give any secret help or comfort, it is not well known. Yet this is manifest, that when they were convinced in open Senate, Cicero, being at that time Consul, asking every man's opinion in the Senate, what punishment they should have, and every one of them till it came to Caesar, gave sentence they should die; Caesar then rising up to speak made an oration (penned and premeditated before), and said that it was neither lawful, nor yet their custom did bear it, to put men of such nobility to death (but in an extremity) without lawful indictment and condemnation. And therefore, that if they were put in prison in some city of Italy, where Cicero thought best, until that Catiline were overthrown, the Senate then might at their pleasure quietly take such order therein, as might best appear unto their wisdoms. This opinion was thought more gentle, and withal was uttered with such a passing good grace and eloquence, that not only they which were to speak after him did approve it, but such also as had spoken to the contrary before revoked their opinion and stuck to his, until it came to Cato and Catulus to speak. They both did sharply inveigh against him, but Cato chiefly: who in his oration made Caesar suspected to be of the conspiracy, and stoutly spake against him, insomuch that the offenders were put into the hands of the officers to be put to death. Caesar coming out of the Senate, a company of young men, which guarded

[marginal notes: Caesar went about to deliver the conspirators. Cato's oration against Caesar.]

Cicero for the safety of his person, did set upon him with their swords drawn. But some say that Curio covered Caesar with his gown, and took him out of their hands. And Cicero self, when the young men looked upon him, beckoned with his head that they should not kill him, either fearing the fury of the people, or else that he thought it too shameful and wicked a part. But, if that were true, I marvel why Cicero did not put it into his book he wrote of his Consulship. But certainly they blamed him afterwards, for that he took not the opportunity offered him against Caesar, only for overmuch fear of the people, that loved him very dearly. For shortly after, when Caesar went into the Senate, to clear himself of certain presumptions and false accusations objected against him, and being bitterly taunted among them, the Senate keeping him lenger than they were wont : the people came about the council house, and called out aloud for him, bidding them let him out. Cato then, fearing the insurrection of the poor needy persons, which were they that put all their hope in Caesar, and did also move the people to stir, did persuade the Senate to make a frank distribution of corn unto them for a month. This distribution did put the commonwealth to a new charge of five hundred and fifty myriads. This counsel quenched a present great fear, and did in happy time scatter and disperse abroad the best part of Caesar's force and power, at such time as he was made Praetor, and that for respect of his office he was most to be feared. Yet all the time he was

JULIUS CAESAR

officer he never sought any alteration in the commonwealth, but contrarily he himself had a great misfortune fell in his own house, which was this. There was a young nobleman of the order of the Patricians, called Publius Clodius, who lacked neither wealth nor eloquence, but otherwise as insolent and impudent a person as any was else in Rome. He became in love with Pompeia, Caesar's wife, who misliked not withal: *The love of P. Clodius unto Pompeia, Caesar's wife.* notwithstanding she was so straitly looked to, and that Aurelia (Caesar's mother), an honest gentlewoman, had such an eye of her, that these two lovers could not meet as they would, without great peril and difficulty. The Romans do use to honour a goddess which they call the good goddess, as the Grecians have her whom they call Gynaeceia, to wit, the goddess of women. Her the Phrygians do claim to *The good goddess, what she was, and her sacrifices.* be peculiar unto them, saying that she is King Midas' mother. Howbeit the Romans hold opinion, that it is a nymph of wood married unto god Faunus. The Grecians, they say also that she was one of the mothers of the god Bacchus, whom they dare not name. And for proof hereof, on her feast day, the women make certain tabernacles of vine twigs and leaves of vine branches, and also they make, as the tale goeth, a holy dragon for this goddess, and do set it by her: besides, it is not lawful for any man to be present at their sacrifices, no not within the house itself where they are made. Furthermore, they say

JULIUS CAESAR

that the women in these sacrifices do many things amongst themselves, much like unto the ceremonies of Orpheus. Now when the time of this feast came, the husband (whether he were Praetor or Consul) and all his men and the boys in the house do come out of it, and leave it wholly to his wife, to order the house at her pleasure, and there the sacrifices and ceremonies are done the most part of the night, and they do besides pass the night away in songs and music. Pompeia, Caesar's wife, being that year to celebrate this feast, Clodius, who had yet no hair on his face, and thereby thought he should not be bewrayed, disguised himself in a singing wench's apparel, because his face was very like unto a young wench. He finding the gates open, being secretly brought in by her chambermaid that was made privy unto it, she left him, and ran to Pompeia her mistress, to tell her that he was come. The chambermaid tarried long before she came again, insomuch as Clodius being weary waiting for her where she left him, he took his pleasure, and went from one place to another in the house, which had very large rooms in it, still shunning the light, and was by chance met withal by one of Aurelia's maids, who, taking him for a woman, prayed her to play. Clodius refusing to play, the maid pulled him forward, and asked him what he was: Clodius then answered her, that he tarried for Abra one of Pompeia's women. So Aurelia's maid, knowing him by his voice, ran straight where the lights and ladies were, and cried out, that there was a man disguised in woman's apparel. The women therewith were so amazed, that Aurelia caused them presently to leave off the ceremonies of the sacrifice, and to hide their secret things, and, having seen the gates fast locked, went immediately up and down the house with torch light to seek out this man: who at the last was found out in the chamber of Pompeia's maid, with whom he hid himself. Thus Clodius being found out, and known of the women, they thrust him out of the doors by the shoulders. The same night the women told their husbands of this chance as soon as they came home. The next morning, there ran a great rumour through the city, how Clodius had attempted a great villany and that he deserved, not only to be punished of them whom he had slandered, but also of the commonwealth and the gods. There was one of the Tribunes of the people that did indict him, and accuse him of high treason to the gods. Furthermore, there were also of the chiefest of the nobility and the Senate, that came to depose against him, and burdened him with many horrible and detestable facts, and specially with incest committed with his own sister, which was married unto Lucullus. Notwithstanding, the people stoutly defended Clodius against their accusations: and this did help him much against the judges, which were amazed, and afraid to stir the people. This notwithstanding, Caesar presently put his wife away, and thereupon, being brought

Clodius taken in the sacrifices of the good goddess.

Clodius accused for profaning the sacrifices of the good goddess.

by Clodius' accuser to be a witness against him, he answered, he knew nothing of that they objected against Clodius. This answer being clean contrary to their expectation that heard it, the accuser asked Caesar, why then he had put away his wife: "Because I will not," said he, "that my wife be so much as suspected." And some say that Caesar spake truly as he thought. But others think that he did it to please the common people, who were very desirous to save Clodius. So Clodius was discharged of this accusation, because the most part of the judges gave a confused judgement, for the fear they stood one way of the danger of the common people if they condemned him, and for the ill opinion of th' other side of the nobility if they did quit him. The government of the province of Spain being fallen unto Caesar for that he was Praetor, his creditors came and cried out upon him, and were importunate of him to be paid. Caesar, being unable to satisfy them, was compelled to go unto Crassus, who was the richest man of all Rome, and that stood in need of Caesar's boldness and courage to withstand Pompey's greatness in the commonwealth. Crassus became his surety unto his greediest creditors for the sum of eight hundred and thirty talents: whereupon they suffered Caesar to depart to the government of his province. In his journey it is reported that,

Caesar putteth away his wife Pompeia.

Clodius quit by the judges for profaning the sacrifices of the good goddess.

Caesar Praetor of Spain.

Crassus surety for Caesar to his creditors.

JULIUS CAESAR

passing over the mountains of the Alps, they came through a little poor village that had not many households, and yet poor cottages. There, his friends that did accompany him asked him merrily, if there were any contending for offices in that town, and whether there were any strife there amongst the noblemen for honour. Caesar, speaking in good earnest, answered: 'I cannot tell that,' said he, 'but for my part, I had rather be the chiefest man here, than the second person in Rome.' Another time also when he was in Spain, reading the history of Alexander's acts, when he had read it, he was sorrowful a good while after, and then burst out in weeping. His friends seeing that, marvelled what should be the cause of his sorrow. He answered them, 'Do ye not think,' said he, 'that I have good cause to be heavy, when King Alexander, being no older than myself is now, had in old time won so many nations and countries: and that I hitherunto have done nothing worthy of myself?' Therefore, when he was come into Spain, he was very careful of his business, and had in few days joined ten new ensigns more of footmen unto the other twenty which he had before. Then, marching forward against the Calaïcans and Lusitanians, he conquered all, and went as far as the great sea Oceanus, subduing all the people which before knew not the Romans for their Lords. There he took order for pacifying of the war, and did as wisely take order for the establishing of peace. For he did reconcile the cities together, and made them friends

Caesar's acts in Spain.

one with another, but specially he pacified all suits of law and strife betwixt the debtors and creditors, which grew by reason of usury. For he ordained that the creditors should take yearly two parts of the revenue of their debtors, until such time as they had paid themselves: and that the debtors should have the third part to themselves to live withal. He, having won great estimation by this good order taken, returned from this government very rich, and his soldiers also full of rich spoils, who called him Imperator, to say, sovereign captain. Now the Romans having a custom, that such as demanded honour of triumph should remain a while without the city, and that they on th' other side which sued for the Consulship should of necessity be there in person: Caesar coming unhappily at that very time when the Consuls were chosen, he sent to pray the Senate to do him that favour, that, being absent, he might by his friends sue for the Consulship. Cato at the first did vehemently inveigh against it, vouching an express law forbidding the contrary. But afterwards perceiving that notwithstanding the reasons he alleged, many of the Senators (being won by Caesar) favoured his request, yet he cunningly sought all he could to prevent them, prolonging time, dilating his oration until night. Caesar thereupon determined rather to give over the suit of his triumph, and to make suit for the Consulship: and so came into the city, and had such a device with him, as went beyond them all

Caesar's order betwixt the creditor and debtor.

Caesar's soldiers called him Imperator.

but Cato only. His device was this. Pompey and Crassus, two of the greatest personages of the city of Rome, being at jar together, Caesar made them friends, and by that means got unto himself the power of them both: for by colour of that gentle act and friendship of his he subtly (unwares to them all) did greatly alter and change the state of the commonwealth. For it was not the private discord between Pompey and Caesar, as many men thought, that caused the civil war: but rather it was their agreement together, who joined all their powers first to overthrow the state of the Senate and nobility, and afterwards they fell at jar one with another. But Cato, that then foresaw and prophesied many times what would follow, was taken but for a vain man: but afterwards they found him a wiser man, than happy in his counsel. Thus Caesar being brought unto the assembly of the election in the midst of these two noble persons whom he had before reconciled together: he was there chosen Consul, with Calphurnius Bibulus, without gainsaying or contradiction of any man. Now, when he was entered into his office, he began to put forth laws meeter for a seditious Tribune of the people than for a Consul: because by them he preferred the division of lands, and distributing of corn to every citizen, *gratis*, to please them withal. But when the noblemen of the Senate were against his device, he desiring no better occasion

Caesar reconcileth Pompey and Crassus together.

Cato's foresight and prophecy.

Caesar's first consulship with Calphurnius Bibulus.

Caesar's laws.

began to cry out and to protest, that by the overhardness and austerity of the Senate they drave him against his will to lean unto the people : and thereupon having Crassus on th' one side of him, and Pompey on th' other, he asked them openly in th' assembly, if they did give their consent unto the laws which he had put forth. They both answered, they did. Then he prayed them to stand by him against those that threatened him with force of sword to let him. Crassus gave him his word, he would. Pompey also did the like, and added thereunto, that he would come with his sword and target both against them that would withstand him with their swords. These words offended much the Senate, being far unmeet for his gravity, and undecent for the majesty and honour he carried, and most of all uncomely for the presence of the Senate whom he should have reverenced : and were speeches fitter for a rash light-headed youth than for his person. Howbeit the common people on th' other side, they rejoiced. Then Caesar, because he would be more assured of Pompey's power and friendship, he gave him his daughter Julia in marriage, which was made sure before unto Servilius Caepio, and promised him in exchange Pompey's daughter, the which was sure also unto Faustus the son of Sylla. And shortly after also, Caesar self did marry Calphurnia, the daughter of Piso, whom he caused to be made Consul to succeed him the next year following. Cato then cried out with

Lex agraria.

Caesar married his daughter Julia unto Pompey.

Caesar married Calphurnia, the daughter of Piso.

JULIUS CAESAR

open mouth, and called the gods to witness, that it was a shameful matter, and not to be suffered, that they should in that sort make havoc of the Empire of Rome, by such horrible bawdy matches, distributing among themselves through those wicked marriages the governments of the provinces and of great armies. Calphurnius Bibulus, fellow Consul with Caesar, perceiving that he did contend in vain, making all the resistance he could to withstand this law, and that oftentimes he was in danger to be slain with Cato in the market-place and assembly: he kept close in his house all the rest of his Consulship. When Pompey had married Julia, he filled all the market-place with soldiers, and by open force authorised the laws which Caesar made in the behalf of the people. *Pompey by force of arms authorised Caesar's laws.* Furthermore, he procured that Caesar had Gaul on this side and beyond the Alps, and all Illyria, with four legions, granted him for five years. Then Cato standing up to speak against it, Caesar bade his officers lay hold of him, and carry him to prison, thinking he would *Caesar sent Cato to prison.* have appealed unto the Tribunes. But Cato said never a word, when he went his way. Caesar perceiving then, that not only the Senators and nobility were offended, but that the common people also, for the reverence they bare unto Cato's virtues, were ashamed, and went away with silence: he himself secretly did pray one of the Tribunes that he would take Cato from the officers. But after he had played this part, there were few Senators that would be

President of the Senate under him, but left the city, because they could not away with his doings. And of them there was an old man called Considius, that on a time boldly told him the rest durst not come to council, because they were afraid of his soldiers. Caesar answered him again: 'And why then dost not thou keep thee at home for the same fear?' Considius replied, 'Because my age taketh away fear from me: for, having so short a time to live, I have no care to prolong it further.' The shamefullest part that Caesar played while he was Consul seemeth to be this: when he chose P. Clodius Tribune of the people, that had offered his wife such dishonour, and profaned the holy ancient mysteries of the women, which were celebrated in his own house. Clodius sued to be Tribune to no other end but to destroy Cicero: and Caesar self also departed not from Rome to his army before he had set them together by the ears, and driven Cicero out of Italy. All these things they say he did, before the wars with the Gauls. But the time of the great armies and conquests he made afterwards, and of the war in the which he subdued all the Gauls (entering into another course of life far contrary unto the first), made him to be known for as valiant a soldier and as excellent a captain to lead men, as those that afore him had been counted the wisest and most valiantest generals that ever were, and that by their valiant deeds had achieved great honour. For whosoever would compare the

Caesar by Clodius drave Cicero out of Italy.

Caesar a valiant soldier and a skilful captain.

house of the Fabians, of the Scipios, of the Metellians, yea those also of his own time, or long before him, as Sylla, Marius, the two Lucullians, and Pompey self,

> Whose fame ascendeth up unto the heavens:

it will appear that Caesar's prowess and deeds of arms did excel them all together. The one, in the hard countries where he made wars: another, in enlarging the realms and countries which he joined unto the Empire of Rome: another, in the multitude and power of his enemies whom he overcame: another, in the rudeness and austere nature of men with whom he had to do, whose manners afterwards he softened and made civil: another, in courtesy and clemency which he used unto them whom he had conquered: another, in great bounty and liberality bestowed upon them that served under him in those wars: and in fine, he excelled them all in the number of battles he had fought, and in the multitude of his enemies he had slain in battle. For in less than ten years' war in Gaul he took by force and assault above eight hundred towns: he conquered three hundred several nations: and having before him in battle thirty hundred thousand soldiers, at sundry times he slew ten hundred thousand of them, and took as many more prisoners. Furthermore, he was so entirely beloved of his soldiers, that to do him service (where otherwise they were no more than other men in any private

Caesar's conquests in Gaul.

The love and respect of Caesar's soldiers unto him.

quarrel) if Caesar's honour were touched, they were invincible, and would so desperately venture themselves, and with such fury, that no man was able to abide them. And this appeareth plainly by the example of Acilius: who, in a battle by sea before the city of Marseilles, boarding one of his enemies ships, one cut off his right hand with a sword, but yet he forsook not his target which he had in his left hand, but thrust it in his enemies faces, and made them fly, so that he won their ship from them. And Cassius Scaeva also, in a conflict before the city of Dyrrachium, having one of his eyes put out with an arrow, his shoulder stricken through with a dart, and his thigh with another, and having received thirty arrows upon his shield: he called to his enemies, and made as though he would yield unto them. But when two of them came running to him, he clave one of their shoulders from his body with his sword, and hurt the other in the face: so that he made him turn his back, and at the length saved himself, by means of his companions that came to help him. And in Britain also, when the captains of the bands were driven into a marish or bog full of mire and dirt, and that the enemies did fiercely assail them there: Caesar then standing to view the battle, he saw a private soldier of his thrust in among the captains, and fought so valiantly in their defence that at the length he drave the barbarous people to fly and by his means saved the captains, which otherwise were in great danger to have been

The wonderful valiantness of Acilius, Cassius Scaeva, and divers others of Caesar's soldiers.

cast away. Then this soldier, being the hindmost man of all the captains, marching with great pain through the mire and dirt, half swimming and half afoot, in the end got to the other side, but left his shield behind him. Caesar, wondering at his noble courage, ran to him with joy to embrace him. But the poor soldier hanging down his head, the water standing in his eyes, fell down at Caesar's feet, and besought him to pardon him, for that he had left his target behind him. And in Africk also, Scipio having taken one of Caesar's ships, and Granius Petronius aboard on her amongst other, not long before chosen treasurer: he put all the rest to the sword but him, and said he would give him his life. But Petronius answered him again: that Caesar's soldiers did not use to have their lives given them, but to give others their lives: and with those words he drew his sword, and thrust himself through. Now Caesar's self did breed this noble courage and life in them. First, for that he gave them bountifully, and did honour them also, shewing thereby, that he did not heap up riches in the wars to maintain his life afterwards in wantonness and pleasure, but that he did keep it in store, honourably to reward their valiant service: and that by so much he thought himself rich, by how much he was liberal in rewarding of them that had deserved it. Furthermore, they did not wonder so much at his valiantness in putting himself at every instant in such manifest danger, and in taking so extreme pains as he did, knowing that it was his

<small>Granius Petronius.</small>

greedy desire of honour that set him afire, and pricked him forward to do it: but that he always continued all labour and hardness, more than his body could bear, that filled them all with admiration. For concerning the constitution of his body, he was lean, white, and soft skinned, and often subject to headache, and otherwhile to the falling sickness, (the which took him the first time, as it is reported, in Corduba, a city of Spain): but yet therefore yielded not to the disease of his body, to make it a cloak to cherish him withal, but contrarily took the pains of war as a medicine to cure his sick body, fighting always with his disease, travelling continually, living soberly, and commonly lying abroad in the field. For the most nights he slept in his coach or litter, and thereby bestowed his rest, to make him always able to do something: and in the daytime, he would travel up and down the country to see towns, castles, and strong places. He had always a secretary with him in his coach, who did still write as he went by the way, and a soldier behind him that carried his sword. He made such speed the first time he came from Rome, when he had his office, that in eight days he came to the river of Rhone. He was so excellent a rider of horse from his youth that, holding his hands behind him, he would gallop his horse upon the spur. In his wars in Gaul, he did further exercise himself to indite letters as he rode by the way, and did occupy two secretaries at once with as much as they could write: and, as Oppius writeth, more than two at a time.

Caesar had the falling sickness

And it is reported, that Caesar was the first that devised friends might talk together by writing ciphers in letters, when he had no leisure to speak with them for his urgent business, and for the great distance besides from Rome. How little accompt Caesar made of his diet, this example doth prove it. Caesar supping one night in Milan with his friend Valerius Leo, there was served sperage to his board, and oil of perfume put into it instead of salad oil. He simply ate it, and found no fault, blaming his friends that were offended: and told them, that it had been enough for them to have abstained to eat of that they misliked, and not to shame their friend, and how that he lacked good manner that found fault with his friend. Another time as he travelled through the country, he was driven by foul weather on the sudden to take a poor man's cottage, that had but one little cabin in it, and that was so narrow, that one man could but scarce lie in it. Then he said to his friends that were about him: 'Greatest rooms are meetest for greatest men, and the most necessary rooms for the sickest persons.' And thereupon he caused Oppius that was sick to lie there all night: and he himself, with the rest of his friends, lay without doors, under the easing of the house. The first war that Caesar made with the Gauls was with the Helvetians and Tigurinians, who, having set fire of all their good cities, to the number of twelve, and four hundred villages besides, came to invade that part of Gaul which was

The temperance of Caesar in his diet.

Caesar's civility not to blame his friend.

subject to the Romans, as the Cimbri and Teutons had done before: unto whom for valiantness they gave no place, and they were also a great number of them (for they were three hundred thousand souls in all) whereof there were a hundred four-score and ten thousand fighting men. Of those, it was not Caesar himself that overcame the Tigurinians, but Labienus his Lieutenant, that overthrew them by the river of Arar. But the Helvetians themselves came suddenly with their army to set upon him, as he was going towards a city of his confederates. Caesar, perceiving that, made haste to get him some place of strength, and there did set his men in battle ray. When one brought him his horse to get up on which he used in battle, he said unto them: 'When I have overcome mine enemies, I will then get up on him to follow the chase, but now let us give them charge.' Therewith he marched forward afoot, and gave charge: and there fought it out a long time, before he could make them fly that were in battle. But the greatest trouble he had was to distress their camp, and to break their strength which they had made with their carts. For there they that before had fled from the battle did not only put themselves in force, and valiantly fought it out: but their wives and children also fighting for their lives to the death were all slain, and the battle was scant ended at midnight. Now if the act of this victory was famous, unto that he also added

The Tigurinians slain by Labienus. Arar fl.

Caesar refused his horse when he fought a battle.

The Helvetians slain by Caesar.

JULIUS CAESAR

another as notable, or exceeding it. For of all the barbarous people that had escaped from this battle he gathered together again above a hundred thousand of them, and compelled them to return home into their country which they had forsaken, and unto their towns also which they had burnt : because he feared the Germans would come over the river of Rhine, and occupy that country lying void. The second war he made was in defence of the Gauls against the Germans : although before he himself had caused Ariovistus their king to be received for a confederate of the Romans. Notwithstanding, they were grown very unquiet neighbours, and it appeared plainly that, having any occasion offered them to enlarge their territories, they would not content them with their own, but meant to invade and possess the rest of Gaul Caesar perceiving that some of his captains trembled for fear, but specially the young gentlemen of noble houses of Rome, who thought to have gone to the wars with him as only for their pleasure and gain · he called them to council, and commanded them that were afraid, that they should depart home, and not put themselves in danger against their wills, sith they had such womanish faint hearts to shrink when he had need of them. And for himself, he said, he would set upon the barbarous people, though he had left him but the tenth legion only, saying that the enemies were no valianter than the Cimbri had been, nor that he was a captain inferior unto Marius. This oration being made,

Rhenus fl.

Caesar made war with King Ariovistus

the soldiers of the tenth legion sent their lieutenants unto him, to thank him for the good opinion he had of them: and the other legions also fell out with their captains, and all of them together followed him many days' journey with good will to serve him, until they came within two hundred furlongs of the camp of the enemies. Ariovistus' courage was well cooled, when he saw Caesar was come, and that the Romans came to seek out the Germans, where they thought and made accompt that they durst not have abidden them: and therefore, nothing mistrusting it would have come so to pass, he wondered much at Caesar's courage, and the more when he saw his own army in a maze withal. But much more did their courages fall by reason of the foolish women prophesiers they had among them, which did foretell things to come: who, considering the waves and trouble of the rivers, and the terrible noise they made running down the stream, did forewarn them not to fight until the new moon. Caesar having intelligence thereof, and perceiving that the barbarous people thereupon stirred not, thought it best then to set upon them, being discouraged with this superstitious fear, rather than, losing time, he should tarry their leisure. So he did skirmish with them even to their forts and little hills where they lay, and by this means provoked them so, that with great fury they came down to fight. There he overcame them in battle, and followed them in chase, with great slaughter, three hundred furlong,

The wise women of Germany, how they did foretell things to come.

JULIUS CAESAR

even unto the river of Rhine : and he filled all the fields thitherto with dead bodies and spoils. Howbeit Ariovistus, flying with speed, got over the river of Rhine, and escaped with a few of his men. It is said that there were slain four-score thousand persons at this battle. *King Ariovistus overthrown by Caesar.* After this exploit, Caesar left his army amongst the Sequanes to winter there : and he himself in the meantime, thinking of th' affairs at Rome, went over the mountains into Gaul about the river of Po, being part of his province which he had in charge. For there the river called Rubico divideth the rest of Italy from Gaul on this side the Alps. Caesar lying there did practise to make friends in Rome, because many came thither to see him : unto whom he granted their suits they demanded, and sent them home also, partly with liberal rewards, and partly with large promises and hope. Now, during all this conquest of the Gauls, Pompey did not consider how Caesar interchangeably did conquer the Gauls with the weapons of the Romans, and won the Romans again with the money of the Gauls. Caesar being advertised that the Belgae (which were the warlikest men of all the Gauls, and that occupied the third part of Gaul) were all up in arms, and had raised a great power of men together : he straight made towards them with all possible speed, and found them spoiling and over-running the country of the Gauls, their neighbours, and confederates of the Romans. *The Belgae overcome by Caesar.* So he gave them battle, and, they fighting cowardly, he overthrew the most part of them which were in a troop together, and slew such a number of them, that the Romans passed over deep rivers and lakes afoot upon their dead bodies, the rivers were so full of them. After this overthrow, they that dwelt nearest unto the seaside, and were next neighbours unto the ocean, did yield themselves without any compulsion or fight: whereupon, he led his army against the Nervians, the stoutest warriors of all the Belgae. They, dwelling in the wood country, had conveyed their wives, children, and goods into a marvellous great forest, as far from their enemies as they could: and being about the number of six-score thousand fighting men and more, they came one day and set upon Caesar, when his army was out of order, and fortifying of his camp, little looking to have fought that day. At the first charge they brake the horsemen of the Romans, and compassing in the twelfth and seventh legion, they slew all the centurions and captains of the bands. And had not Caesar self taken his shield on his arm, and, flying in amongst the barbarous people, made a lane through them that fought before him. and the tenth legion also, seeing him in danger, run unto him from the top of the hill where they stood in battle, and broken the ranks of their enemies: there had not a Roman escaped alive that day. But, taking example of Caesar's valiantness, they fought desperately beyond their power, and yet could not make the Nervians fly, but they fought it out to the death,

Nervii the stoutest warriors of all the Belgae.

JULIUS CAESAR

till they were all in manner slain in the field. It is written that of three-score thousand fighting men there escaped only but five hundred : and of four hundred gentlemen and counsellors of the Romans but three saved. *The Nervii slain by Caesar.* The Senate understanding it at Rome ordained that they should do sacrifice unto the gods, and keep feasts and solemn processions fifteen days together without intermission, having never made the like ordinance at Rome for any victory that ever was obtained. Because they saw the danger had been marvellous great, so many nations rising as they did in arms together against him : and further, the love of the people unto him made his victory much more famous. For when Caesar had set his affairs at a stay in Gaul on the other side of the Alps, he always used to lie about the river of Po in the winter-time, to give direction for the establishing of things at Rome at his pleasure. For not only they that made suit for offices at Rome were chosen magistrates by means of Caesar's money which he gave them, with the which bribing the people they bought their voices, and when they were in office did all that they could to increase Caesar's power and greatness : but the greatest and chiefest men also of the nobility went unto Luca unto him. As Pompey, Crassus, Appius, Praetor of Sardinia, and Nepos, Proconsul in Spain. *The great lords of Rome came to Luca to Caesar.* Insomuch that there were at one time six-score sergeants carrying rods and axes before the magistrates : and above two hundred Senators besides. There they fell in consultation, and determined that Pompey and Crassus should again be chosen Consuls the next year following. Furthermore, they did appoint that Caesar should have money again delivered him to pay his army and beside did prorogue the time of his government five years further. This was thought a very strange and an unreasonable matter unto wise men. For they themselves that had taken so much money of Caesar persuaded the Senate to let him have money of the common treasure, as though he had had none before : yea, to speak more plainly they compelled the Senate unto it, sighing and lamenting to see the decrees they passed. Cato was not there then, for they had purposely sent him before into Cyprus. Howbeit Favonius, that followed Cato's steps, when he saw that he could not prevail, nor withstand them : he went out of the Senate in choler, and cried out amongst the people that it was a horrible shame. But no man did hearken to him, some for the reverence they bare unto Pompey and Crassus, and others, favouring Caesar's proceedings, did put all their hope and trust in him : and therefore did quiet themselves, and stirred not. Then Caesar, returning into Gaul beyond the Alps unto his army, found there a great war in the country. For two great nations of Germany had not long before passed over the river of Rhine, to conquer new lands : and the one of these people were called Ipes, and the other Tenterides. Now touching the battle which Caesar fought with them, he

Ipes & Tenterides, people of Germany.

JULIUS CAESAR

himself doth describe it in his commentaries in this sort. That the barbarous people having sent ambassadors unto him, to require peace for a certain time, they notwithstanding, against law of arms, came and set upon him as he travelled by the way, insomuch as eight hundred of their men of arms overthrew five thousand of his horsemen, who nothing at all mistrusted their coming. *Caesar's horsemen put to flight.* Again, that they sent him other ambassadors to mock him once more : but that he kept them, and therewith caused his whole army to march against them, thinking it a folly and madness to keep faith with such traitorous barbarous breakers of leagues. Canutius writeth that the Senate appointing again to do new sacrifice, processions, and feasts, to give thanks to the gods for this victory, Cato was of contrary opinion, that Caesar should be delivered into the hands of the barbarous people, for to purge their city and commonwealth of this breach of faith, and to turn the curse upon him that was the author of it. Of these barbarous people which came over the Rhine, (being about the number of four hundred thousand persons), they were all in manner slain, saving a *The Ipes and Tenterides slain by Caesar.* very few of them, that flying from the battle got over the river of Rhine again, who were received by the Sicambrians, another people of the Germans. Caesar taking this occasion against them, lacking no good will of himself besides, to have the honour to be counted the first Roman that ever passed over the river of Rhine *Sicambri, a people of the Germans.*

with an army: he built a bridge over it. This river is
marvellous broad, and runneth with great fury.
And in that place specially where he built his
bridge, for there it is of a great breadth from one
side to th' other, and it hath so strong and swift a
stream besides, that men, casting down great bodies of trees
into the river (which the stream bringeth down with it),
did with the great blows and force thereof marvellously
shake the posts of the bridge he had set up. But to prevent
the blows of those trees, and also to break the fury of the
stream, he made a pile of great wood above the bridge a
good way, and did forcibly ram them into the bottom of
the river, so that in ten days' space he had set up and
finished his bridge of the goodliest carpenter's work, and
most excellent invention to see to, that could be possibly
thought or devised. Then, passing over his army upon it,
he found none that durst any more fight with him. For
the Suevians, which were the warlikest people of all
Germany, had gotten themselves with their goods into
wonderful great valleys and bogs, full of woods and forests.
Now when he had burnt all the country of his enemies, and
confirmed the league with the confederates of the Romans,
he returned back again into Gaul after he had tarried eighteen days at the most in Germany, on th' other side of the Rhine. The journey he made also into England was a noble enterprise, and very commendable. For he was the first that sailed the west Ocean

Caesar made a bridge over the river of Rhine

Caesar's journey into England.

JULIUS CAESAR

with an army by sea, and that passed through the sea Atlanticum with his army, to make war in that so great and famous Island: (which many ancient writers would not believe that it was so indeed, and did make them vary about it, saying that it was but a fable and a lie): and was the first that enlarged the Roman Empire beyond the earth inhabitable. For twice he passed over the narrow sea against the firm land of Gaul, and fighting many battles there, did hurt his enemies more than enrich his own men: because of men hardly brought up and poor there was nothing to be gotten. Whereupon his war had not such success as he looked for: and therefore, taking pledges only of the king, and imposing a yearly tribute upon him, to be paid unto the people of Rome, he returned again into Gaul. There he was no sooner landed, but he found letters ready to be sent over the sea unto him: in the which he was advertised from Rome of the death of his daughter, that she was dead with child by Pompey. For the which Pompey and Caesar both were marvellous sorrowful: and their friends mourned also, thinking that this alliance, which maintained the commonwealth (that otherwise was very tickle) in good peace and concord, was now severed and broken asunder, and the rather likely, because the child lived not long after the mother. So the common people at Rome took the corpse of Julia, in despite of the Tribunes, and buried it in the field of Mars. Now Caesar being driven to divide his army

The death of Julia, Caesar's daughter

(that was very great) into sundry garrisons for the winter-time, and returning again into Italy as he was wont: all Gaul rebelled again, and had raised great armies in every quarter to set upon the Romans, and to assay if they could distress their forts where they lay in garrison. The greatest number and most war-like men of these Gauls that entered into action of rebellion were led by one Ambiorix: and first did set upon the garrisons of Cotta and Titurius, whom they slew and all the soldiers they had about them. Then they went with three-score thousand fighting men to besiege the garrison which Quintus Cicero had in his charge, and had almost taken them by force, because all the soldiers were every man of them hurt: but they were so valiant and courageous, that they did more than men (as they say) in defending of themselves. These news being come to Caesar, who was far from thence at that time, he returned with all possible speed, and levying seven thousand soldiers made haste to help Cicero that was in such distress. The Gauls that did besiege Cicero, understanding of Caesar's coming, raised their siege incontinently, to go and meet him: making accompt that he was but a handful in their hands, they were so few. Caesar, to deceive them, still drew back, and made as though he fled from them, lodging in places meet for a captain that had but a few to fight with a great number of his enemies, and commanded his men in nowise to stir out to skirmish with them, but compelled them to

JULIUS CAESAR 39

raise up the rampers of his camp and to fortify the gates, as men that were afraid, because the enemies should the less esteem of them : until that at length he took opportunity by their disorderly coming to assail the trenches of his camp, (they were grown to such a presumptuous boldness and bravery), and then sallying out upon them he put them all to flight with slaughter of a great number of them. This did suppress all the rebellions of the Gauls in those parts, and furthermore, he himself in person went in the midst of winter thither, where he heard they did rebel : for that there was come a new supply out of Italy of three whole legions in their room which he had lost : of the which, two of them Pompey lent him, and the other legion he himself had levied in Gaul about the river of Po. During these stirs brake forth the beginning of the greatest and most dangerous war that he had in all Gaul, the which had been secretly practised of long time by the chiefest and most warlike people of that country, who had levied a wonderful great power. For everywhere they levied multitudes of men, and great riches besides, to fortify their strongholds. Furthermore, the country where they rose was very ill to come unto, and specially at that time being winter, when the rivers were frozen, the woods and forests covered with snow, the meadows drowned with floods, and the fields so deep of snow, that no ways were to be found, neither the marishes nor rivers to be discerned, all was so

Caesar slew the Gauls led by Ambiorix.

The second rebellion of the Gauls against Caesar.

overflown and drowned with water: all which troubles together were enough (as they thought) to keep Caesar from setting upon the rebels. Many nations of the Gauls were of this conspiracy, but two of the chiefest were the Arvernians and Carnutes: who had chosen Vercingetorix for their Lieutenant general, whose father the Gauls before had put to death, because they thought he aspired to make himself king. This Vercingetorix, dividing his army into divers parts, and appointing divers captains over them, had gotten to take his part all the people and countries thereabout, even as far as they that dwell towards the sea *Adriatic, having further determined (understanding that Rome did conspire against Caesar) to make all Gaul rise in arms against him. So that if he had but tarried a little lenger until Caesar had entered into his civil wars, he had put all Italy in as great fear and danger, as it was when the Cimbri did come and invade it. But Caesar, that was very valiant in all assays and dangers of war, and that was very skilful to take time and opportunity: so soon as he understood the news of the rebellion, he departed with speed, and returned back the self same way which he had gone, making the barbarous people know that they should deal with an army unvincible, and which they could not possibly withstand, considering the great speed he had made with the same in so sharp and hard a winter. For where they

<small>Vercingetorix captain of the rebels against Caesar.</small>

<small>*Some say that in this place is to be read in the Greek πρὸς τὸν Ἄραριν, which is the river Saone.</small>

JULIUS CAESAR

would not possibly have believed that a post or currer could have come in so short a time from the place where he was unto them, they wondered when they saw him burning and destroying the country, the towns, and strong forts where he came with his army, taking all to mercy that yielded unto him: until such time as the Aedui took arms against him, who before were wont to be called the brethren of the Romans, and were greatly honoured of them. Wherefore Caesar's men when they understood that they had joined with the rebels, they were marvellous sorry and half discouraged. Thereupon Caesar, departing from those parties, went through the country of the Lingones, to enter the country of the Burgonians,[1] who were confederates of the Romans, and the nearest unto Italy on that side, in respect of all the rest of Gaul. Thither the enemies came to set upon him, and to environ him of all sides with an infinite number of thousands of fighting men. Caesar, on th' other side, tarried their coming, and fighting with them a long time he made them so afraid of him that at length he overcame the barbarous people. But at the first it seemeth notwithstanding that he had received some overthrow: for the Arvernians shewed a sword hanged up in one of their temples, which they said they had won from Caesar. Insomuch as Caesar self, coming that way by occasion, saw it, and fell a-laughing at it. But some of his friends going about to take it away, he would not suffer

The Aedui rebel against the Romans.

Sequani [1]

Vercingetorix overthrown by Caesar.

them, but bade them let it alone and touch it not, for it was a holy thing. Notwithstanding, such as at the first had saved themselves by flying, the most of them were gotten with their king into the city of Alexia, the which Caesar went and besieged, although it seemed inexpugnable, both for the height of the walls, as also for the multitude of soldiers they had to defend it. But now, during this siege, he fell into a marvellous great danger without, almost incredible. For an army of three hundred thousand fighting men of the best men that were among all the nations of the Gauls came against him, being at the siege of Alexia, besides them that were within the city, which amounted to the number of three-score and ten thousand fighting men at the least: so that, perceiving he was shut in betwixt two so great armies, he was driven to fortify himself with two walls, the one against them of the city, and the other against them without. For if those two armies had joined together, Caesar had been utterly undone. And therefore this siege of Alexia, and the battle he won before it, did deservedly win him more honour and fame than any other. For there, in that instant and extreme danger, he shewed more valiantness and wisdom than he did in any battle he fought before. But what a wonderful thing was this! that they of the city never heard anything of them that came to aid them, until Caesar had overcome them: and furthermore, that the Romans them-

The siege of Alexia.

Caesar's danger and wise policy.

Caesar's great victory at Alexia.

JULIUS CAESAR

selves which kept watch upon the wall that was built against the city knew also no more of it than they, but when it was done, and that they heard the cries and lamentations of men and women in Alexia, when they perceived on th' other side of the city such a number of glistering shields of gold and silver, such store of bloody corselets and armours, such a deal of plate and movables, and such a number of tents and pavilions after the fashion of the Gauls, which the Romans had gotten of their spoils in their camp. Thus suddenly was this great army vanished, as a dream or vision : where the most part of them were slain that day in battle. Furthermore, after that they within the city of Alexia had done great hurt to Caesar and themselves also : in the end they all yielded themselves. And Vercingetorix (he that was their king and captain in all this war) went out of the gates excellently well armed, and his horse furnished with rich caparison accordingly, and rode round about Caesar, who sate in his chair of estate. Then lighting from his horse, he took off his caparison and furniture, and unarmed himself, and laid all on the ground, and went and sate down at Caesar's feet, and said never a word. So Caesar at length committed him as a prisoner taken in the wars, to lead him afterwards in his triumph at Rome. Now Caesar had of long time determined to destroy Pompey, and Pompey him also. For Crassus being killed amongst the Parthians, who only did see that one of them two must needs fall, nothing kept

Alexia yielded up to Caesar.

Caesar from being the greatest person, but because he destroyed not Pompey that was the greater: neither did anything let Pompey to withstand that it should not come to pass, but because he did not first overcome Caesar, whom only he feared. For till then Pompey had not long feared him, but always before set light by him, thinking it an easy matter for him to put him down when he would, sith he had brought him to that greatness he was come unto. But Caesar contrarily, having had that drift in his head from the beginning, like a wrestler that studieth for tricks to overthrow his adversary: he went far from Rome to exercise himself in the wars of Gaul, where he did train his army, and presently by his valiant deeds did increase his fame and honour. By these means became Caesar as famous as Pompey in his doings, and lacked no more to put his enterprise in execution but some occasions of colour, which Pompey partly gave him, and partly also the time delivered him, but chiefly the hard fortune and ill government at that time of the commonwealth at Rome. For they that made suit for honour and offices bought the voices of the people with ready money, which they gave out openly to usury without shame or fear. Thereupon the common people that had sold their voices for money came to the market-place at the day of election, to fight for him that had hired them: not with their voices, but with their bows, slings,

The discord betwixt Caesar and Pompey, and the cause of the civil wars.

Caesar's craftiness.

The people's voices bought at Rome for money.

JULIUS CAESAR

and swords. So that the assembly seldom time brake up but that the pulpit for orations was defiled and sprinkled with the blood of them that were slain in the market-place, the city remaining all that time without government of magistrate, like a ship left without a pilot. Insomuch as men of deep judgement and discretion, seeing such fury and madness of the people, thought themselves happy if the commonwealth were no worse troubled, than with the absolute state of a monarchy and sovereign lord to govern them. Furthermore, there were many that were not afraid to speak it openly, that there was no other help to remedy the troubles of the commonwealth, but by the authority of one man only that should command them all: and that this medicine must be ministered by the hands of him that was the gentlest physician, meaning covertly Pompey. Now Pompey used many fine speeches, making semblance as though he would none of it, and yet cunningly underhand did lay all the irons in the fire he could, to bring it to pass, that he might be chosen Dictator. Cato finding the mark he shot at, and fearing lest in the end the people should be compelled to make him Dictator: he persuaded the Senate rather to make him sole Consul, that, contenting himself with that more just and lawful government, he should not covet the other unlawful. The Senate, following his counsel, did not only make him Consul, but further did prorogue his government of the provinces he had. For he had two provinces, all Spain and Africk, the

Pompey governed Spain and Africk

JULIUS CAESAR

which he governed by his Lieutenants: and further he received yearly of the common treasure to pay his soldiers a thousand talents. Hereupon Caesar took occasion also to send his men to make suit in his name for the Consulship, and also to have the government of his provinces prorogued. Pompey at the first held his peace. But Marcellus and Lentulus (that otherwise hated Caesar) withstood them, and to shame and dishonour him, had much needless speech in matters of weight. Furthermore, they took away the freedom from the Colonies which Caesar had lately brought unto the city of Novum Comum in Gaul towards Italy, where Caesar not long before had lodged them. And moreover, when Marcellus was Consul, he made one of the Senators in that city to be whipped with rods, who came to Rome about those matters: and said, he gave him those marks that he should know he was no Roman Citizen, and bade him go his way, and tell Caesar of it. After Marcellus' Consulship, Caesar, setting open his coffers of the treasure he had gotten among the Gauls, did frankly give it out amongst the Magistrates at Rome, without restraint or spare. First, he set Curio the Tribune clear out of debt: and gave also unto Paul the Consul a thousand five hundred talents, with which money he built that notable palace by the market-place, called Paul's Basilick, in the place of Fulvius' Basilick. Then Pompey, being afraid of

Caesar sueth the second time to be Consul, and to have his government prorogued.

Caesar bribeth the Magistrates at Rome.

JULIUS CAESAR

this practice, began openly to procure, both by himself and his friends, that they should send Caesar a successor: and moreover, he sent unto Caesar for his two legions of men of war which he had lent him for the conquest of Gaul. Caesar sent him them again, and gave every private soldier two hundred and fifty silver drachmas. Now they that brought these two legions back from Caesar gave out ill and seditious words against him among the people, and did also abuse Pompey with false persuasions and vain hopes, informing him that he was marvellously desired and wished for in Caesar's camp: and that though in Rome, for the malice and secret spite which the governors there did bear him, he could hardly obtain that *Pompey abused by flatterers* he desired, yet in Gaul he might assure himself, that all the army was at his commandment. They added further also that, if the soldiers there did once return over the mountains again into Italy, they would all straight come to him, they did so hate Caesar. because he wearied them with too much labour and continual fight, and withal, for that they suspected he aspired to be king. These words breeding security in Pompey, and a vain conceit of himself, made him negligent in his doings, so that he made no preparation for war, as though he had no occasion to be afraid, but only studied to thwart Caesar in speech, and to cross the suits he made. Howbeit Caesar passed not of all this. For the report went that one of Caesar's Captains which was sent to Rome to prosecute his suit, being at the Senate door, and hearing that they denied to prorogue Caesar's time of government which he sued for : clapping his hand upon his sword, he said, 'Sith you will not grant it him, this shall give it him.' Notwithstanding, the requests that Caesar propounded carried great semblance of reason with them.

<small>Caesar's requests unto the Senate.</small> For he said that he was contented to lay down arms, so that Pompey did the like : and that both of them as private persons should come and make suit of their Citizens to obtain honourable recompense declaring unto them, that taking arms from him, and granting them unto Pompey, they did wrongfully accuse him in going about to make himself a tyrant, and in the meantime to grant the other means to be a tyrant. Curio making these offers and persuasions openly before the people in the name of Caesar, he was heard with great rejoicing and clapping of hands, and there were some that cast flowers and nosegays upon him when he went his way, as they commonly use to do unto any man, when he hath obtained victory, and won any games. Then Antonius, one of the Tribunes, brought a letter sent from Caesar, and made it openly to be read in despite of the Consuls. But Scipio in the Senate, Pompey's father-in-law, made this motion : that if Caesar did not dismiss his army by a certain day appointed him, the Romans should proclaim him an enemy unto Rome. Then the Consuls openly asked in the presence of the Senators, if they thought it good that Pompey should dismiss his army : but few agreed to that

JULIUS CAESAR 49

demand. After that again they asked, if they liked that Caesar should dismiss his army : thereto they all in manner answered, yea, yea. But when Antonius requested again that both of them should lay down arms : then they were all indifferently of his mind. Notwithstanding, because Scipio did insolently behave himself, and Marcellus also, who cried that they must use force of arms, and not men's opinions, against a thief, the Senate rose straight upon it without further determination, and men changed apparel through the city because of this dissension, as they use to do in a common calamity. After that, there came other letters from Caesar, which seemed much more reasonable : in the which he requested that they would grant him Gaul, that lieth between the mountains of the Alps and Italy, and Illyria, with two legions only, and then that he would request nothing else, until he made suit for the second Consulship. Cicero the Orator, that was newly come from his government of Cilicia, travailed to reconcile them together, and pacified Pompey the best he could : who told him, he would yield to anything he would have him, so he did let him alone with his army. So Cicero persuaded Caesar's friends to be contented to take those two provinces, and six thousand men only, that they might be friends and at peace together. Pompey very willingly yielded unto it and granted them. But Lentulus the Consul would not agree to it, but shamefully drave Curio and Antonius out of the Senate : whereby they themselves gave Caesar a happy

occasion and colour as could be, stirring up his soldiers the
more against them, when he shewed them these
two notable men and Tribunes of the people that
were driven to fly, disguised like slaves, in a carrier's
cart. For they were driven for fear to steal out
of Rome, disguised in that manner. Now at that
time, Caesar had not in all about him above five thousand
footmen, and three thousand horsemen: for the rest of his
army he left on th' other side of the Mountains, to be brought
after him by his Lieutenants. So, considering that for the
execution of his enterprise he should not need so many men
of war at the first, but rather, suddenly stealing upon them,
to make them afraid with his valiantness, taking benefit of
the opportunity of time, because he should more easily make
his enemies afraid of him, coming so suddenly when they
looked not for him, then he should otherwise distress them,
assailing them with his whole army, in giving them leisure
to provide further for him: he commanded his Captains
and Lieutenants to go before, without any other armour
than their swords, to take the city of Ariminum, (a great
city of Gaul, being the first city men come to, when they
come out of Gaul), with as little bloodshed and tumult as
they could possible. Then committing that force and army
he had with him unto Hortensius, one of his friends, he
remained a whole day together, openly in the sight of every
man, to see the sword-players handle their weapons before
him. At night he went into his lodging, and bathing his

Antonius and Curio, Tribunes of the people, fly from Rome to Caesar.

body a little, came afterwards into the hall amongst them, and made merry with them a while whom he had bidden to supper. Then when it was well forward night and very dark, he rose from the table, and prayed his company to be merry, and no man to stir, for he would straight come to them again : howbeit he had secretly before commanded a few of his trustiest friends to follow him, not altogether, but some one way, and some another way. He himself in the meantime took a coach he had hired, and made as though he would have gone some other way at the first, but suddenly he turned back again towards the city of Ariminum. When he was come unto the little river of Rubicon, which divideth Gaul on this side the Alps from Italy, he stayed upon a sudden. For the nearer he came to execute his purpose, the more remorse he had in his conscience, to think what an enterprise he took in hand : and his thoughts also fell out more doubtful, when he entered into consideration of the desperateness of his attempt. So he fell into many thoughts with himself, and spake never a word, waving sometime one way, sometime another way, and oftentimes changed his determination, contrary to himself. So did he talk much also with his friends he had with him, amongst whom was Asinius Pollio, telling them what mischiefs the beginning of this passage over that river would breed in the world, and how much their posterity and them that lived after them would speak of it in time to come. But at length, casting

Caesar's doubtful thoughts at the river of Rubicon.

from him with a noble courage all those perilous thoughts
to come, and speaking these words, which valiant men commonly say that attempt dangerous and desperate enterprises,
'A desperate man feareth no danger, come on!'
he passed over the river, and when he was come
over, he ran with his coach and never stayed, so
that before daylight he was within the city of
Ariminum, and took it. It is said that the night
before he passed over this river he dreamed a
damnable dream, that he carnally knew his mother.
The city of Ariminum being taken, and the
rumour thereof dispersed through all Italy, even
as if it had been open war both by sea and land, and
as if all the Laws of Rome together with th' extreme
bounds and confines of the same had been broken up: a
man would have said, that not only the men and women for
fear, as experience proved at other times, but whole cities
themselves, leaving their habitations, fled from one place to
another through all Italy. And Rome itself also was
immediately filled with the flowing repair of all
the people their neighbours thereabouts, which
came thither from all parties like droves of cattle,
that there was neither officer nor Magistrate that
could any more command them by authority, neither by
any persuasion of reason bridle such a confused and
disorderly multitude: so that Rome had in manner.
destroyed itself for lack of rule and order. For in

The Greek useth this phrase of speech: 'Cast the die.'

Caesar took the city of Ariminum.

Caesar's damnable dream.

Rome in uproar with Caesar's coming.

JULIUS CAESAR

all places men were of contrary opinions, and there were dangerous stirs and tumults everywhere: because they that were glad of this trouble could keep in no certain place, but running up and down the city, when they met with others in divers places, that seemed either to be afraid or angry with this tumult (as otherwise it is impossible in so great a city), they flatly fell out with them, and boldly threatened them with that that was to come. Pompey himself, who at that time was not a little amazed, was yet much more troubled with the ill words some gave him on the one side, and some on the other. For some of them reproved him and said that he had done wisely, and had paid for his folly, because he had made Caesar so great and strong against him and the commonwealth. And other again did blame him, because he had refused the honest offers and reasonable conditions of peace which Caesar had offered him, suffering Lentulus the Consul to abuse him too much. On th' other side, Favonius spake unto him, and bade him stamp on the ground with his foot: for Pompey, being one day in a bravery in the Senate, said openly: let no man take thought for preparation of war, for when he listed, with one stamp of his foot on the ground, he would fill all Italy with soldiers. This notwithstanding, Pompey at that time had greater number of soldiers than Caesar: but they would never let him follow his own determination. For they brought him so many lies, and put so many examples of fear before him, as if Caesar had been already at their heels, and had won all: so that in the end he yielded unto them, and gave place to their fury and madness, determining (seeing all things in such tumult and garboil) that there was no way but to forsake the city, and thereupon commanded the Senate to follow him, and not a man to tarry there, unless he loved tyranny more than his own liberty and the commonwealth. Thus the Consuls themselves, before they had done their common sacrifices accustomed at their going out of the city, fled every man of them. So did likewise the most part of the Senators, taking their own things in haste, such as came first to hand, as if by stealth they had taken them from another. And there were some of them also that always loved Caesar, whose wits were then so troubled and besides themselves with the fear they had conceived, that they also fled and followed the stream of this tumult without manifest cause or necessity. But above all things, it was a lamentable sight to see the city itself, that in this fear and trouble was left at all adventure, as a ship tossed in storm of sea, forsaken of her Pilots, and despairing of her safety. This their departure being thus miserable, yet men esteemed their banishment (for the love they bare unto Pompey) to be their natural country, and reckoned Rome no better than Caesar's camp. At that time also, Labienus, who was one of Caesar's greatest friends, and had been always used as his Lieutenant in the wars of Gaul, and had valiantly fought in his cause, he

Pompey flieth from Rome.

Labienus forsook Caesar, and fled to Pompey.

JULIUS CAESAR

likewise forsook him then, and fled unto Pompey. But Caesar sent his money and carriage after him, and then went and encamped before the city of Corfinium, the which Domitius kept with thirty cohorts or ensigns. When Domitius saw he was besieged, he straight thought himself but undone, and despairing of his success he bade a Physician, a slave of his, give him poison The Physician gave him a drink which he drank, thinking to have died. But shortly after, Domitius, hearing them report what clemency and wonderful courtesy Caesar used unto them he took, repented him then that he had drunk his drink, and began to lament and bewail his desperate resolution taken to die. The Physician did comfort him again, and told him that he had taken a drink only to make him sleep, but not to destroy him. Then Domitius rejoiced, and went straight and yielded himself unto Caesar, who gave him his life: but he notwithstanding stale away immediately, and fled unto Pompey. When these news were brought to Rome, they did marvellously rejoice and comfort them that still remained there: and moreover there were of them that had forsaken Rome, which returned thither again. In the meantime, Caesar did put all Domitius' men in pay, and he did the like through all the cities, where he had taken any Captains that levied men for Pompey. Now Caesar, having assembled a great and dreadful power together, went straight where he thought to find Pompey himself. But Pompey tarried not his coming, but fled into

[margin: Domitius escaped from Caesar, and fled to Pompey.]

the city of Brundusium, from whence he had sent the two Consuls before with that army he had unto Dyrrachium: and he himself also went thither afterwards, when he understood that Caesar was come, as you shall hear more amply hereafter in his life. Caesar lacked no good will to follow him, but wanting ships to take the seas, he returned forthwith to Rome: so that in less than threescore days he was Lord of all Italy, without any bloodshed. Who when he was come to Rome, and found it much quieter than he looked for, and many Senators there also, he courteously entreated them, and prayed them to send unto Pompey, to pacify all matters between them upon reasonable conditions. But no man did attempt it, either because they feared Pompey for that they had forsaken him, or else for that they thought Caesar meant not as he spake, but that they were words of course to colour his purpose withal. And when Metellus also, one of the Tribunes, would not suffer him to take any of the common treasure out of the temple of Saturn, but told him that it was against the law: 'Tush,' said he, 'time of war and law are two things. If this that I do,' quoth he, 'do offend thee, then get thee hence for this time: for war cannot abide this frank and bold speech. But when wars are done, and that we are all quiet again, then thou shalt speak in the pulpit what thou wilt: and yet I do tell thee this of favour, impairing so much my right, for thou art mine, both thou and all them that have risen against me, and whom I have

Pompey flieth into Epirus.

Silent leges inter arma.

JULIUS CAESAR

in my hands.' When he had spoken thus unto Metellus, he went to the temple door where the treasure lay and finding no keys there, he caused smiths to be sent for, and made them break open the locks Metellus thereupon began again to withstand him, and certain men that stood by praised him in his doing: but Caesar at length speaking bigly to him threatened him he would kill him presently, if he troubled him any more: and told him furthermore, 'Young man,' quoth he, 'thou knowest it is harder for me to tell it thee than to do it.' That word made Metellus quake for fear, that he got him away roundly: and ever after that Caesar had all at his commandment for the wars. From thence he went into Spain, to make war with Petreius and Varro, Pompey's Lieutenants: first to get their armies and provinces into his hands which they governed, that afterwards he might follow Pompey the better, leaving never an enemy behind him. In this journey he was oftentimes himself in danger, through the ambushes that were laid for him in divers strange sorts and places, and likely also to have lost all his army for lack of victuals. All this notwithstanding, he never left following of Pompey's Lieutenants, provoking them to battle and intrenching them in: until he had gotten their camp and armies into his hands, albeit that the Lieutenants themselves fled unto Pompey. When Caesar returned again to Rome, Piso his father-in-law gave him counsel to send

[sidenote: Caesar taketh money out of the temple of Saturn.]

[sidenote: Caesar's journey into Spain against Pompey's Lieutenants.]

ambassadors unto Pompey, to treat of peace. But Isauricus, to flatter Caesar, was against it. Caesar, being then created Dictator by the Senate, called home again all the banished men, and restored their children to honour, whose fathers before had been slain in Sylla's time: and did somewhat cut off the usuries that did oppress them, and besides did make some such other ordinances as those, but very few. For he was Dictator but eleven days only, and then did yield it up of himself, and made himself Consul, with Servilius Isauricus, and after that determined to follow the wars. All the rest of his army he left coming on the way behind him, and went himself before with six hundred horse and five legions only of footmen, in the winter quarter, about the month of January, which after the Athenians is called Posideon. Then having passed over the sea Ionium and landed his men, he wan the cities of Oricum and Apollonia. Then he sent his ships back again unto Brundusium, to transport the rest of his soldiers that could not come with that speed he did. They as they came by the way, (like men whose strength of body and lusty youth was decayed), being wearied with so many sundry battles as they had fought with their enemies, complained of Caesar in this sort. 'To what end and purpose doth this man hale us after him up and down the world, using us like slaves and drudges? It is not our armour, but our bodies that bear the

JULIUS CAESAR

blows away: and what, shall we never be without our harness on our backs, and our shields on our arms? Should not Caesar think, at the least when he seeth our blood and wounds, that we are all mortal men, and that we feel the misery and pains that other men do feel? And now, even in the dead of winter, he putteth us unto the mercy of the sea and tempest, yea, which the gods themselves cannot withstand: as if he fled before his enemies, and pursued them not.' Thus spending time with this talk, the soldiers, still marching on, by small journeys came at length unto the city of Brundusium. But when they were come, and found that Caesar had already passed over the sea, then they straight changed their complaints and minds. For they blamed themselves, and took on also with their captains, because they had not made them make more haste in marching: and sitting upon the rocks and cliffs of the sea, they looked over the main sea towards the Realm of Epirus, to see if they could discern the ships returning back to transport them over. Caesar in the meantime being in the city of Apollonia, having but a small army to fight with Pompey, it grieved him for that the rest of his army was so long a-coming, not knowing what way to take. In the end he followed a dangerous determination, to embark unknown in a little pinnace of twelve oars only, to pass over the sea again unto Brundusium: the which he could not do without great danger, considering that all that sea was full of Pompey's ships and armies. So he took ship

A great adventure of Caesar

in the night apparelled like a slave, and went aboard upon this little pinnace, and said never a word, as if he had been some poor man of mean condition. The pinnace lay in the mouth of the river of Anius, the which commonly was wont to be very calm and quiet, by reason of a little wind that came from the shore, which every morning drave back the waves far into the main sea. But that night, by ill fortune, there came a great wind from the sea that overcame the land wind, insomuch as, the force and strength of the river fighting against the violence of the rage and waves of the sea, the encounter was marvellous dangerous, the water of the river being driven back and rebounding upward, with great noise and danger in turning of the water. Thereupon the Master of the pinnace, seeing he could not possibly get out of the mouth of this river, bade the Mariners to cast about again, and to return against the stream. Caesar, hearing that, straight discovered himself unto the Master of the pinnace, who at the first was amazed when he saw him: but Caesar then taking him by the hand said unto him, 'Good fellow, be of good cheer, and forwards hardily, fear not, for thou hast Caesar and his fortune with thee.' Then the Mariners, forgetting the danger of the storm they were in, laid on load with oars and laboured for life what they could against the wind, to get out of the mouth of this river. But at length, perceiving they laboured in vain, and that the pinnace took in abundance of water and was ready to sink: Caesar then to his great

[marginal note: Anius fl.]

JULIUS CAESAR

grief was driven to return back again. Who when he was returned unto his camp, his soldiers came in great companies unto him, and were very sorry that he mistrusted he was not able with them alone to overcome his enemies, but would put his person in danger, to go fetch them that were absent, putting no trust in them that were present. In the meantime Antonius arrived, and brought with him the rest of his army from Brundusium. Then Caesar, finding himself strong enough, went and offered Pompey battle, who was passingly well lodged for victualling of his camp both by sea and land. Caesar on th' other side, who had no great plenty of victuals at the first, was in a very hard case: insomuch as his men gathered roots and mingled them with milk, and ate them. Furthermore, they did make bread of it also, and sometime when they skirmished with the enemies, and came alongst by them that watched and warded, they cast of their bread into their trenches and said that as long as the earth brought forth such fruits, they would never leave besieging of Pompey. But Pompey straightly commanded them that they should neither carry those words nor bread into their camp, fearing lest his men's hearts would fail them, and that they would be afraid, when they should think of their enemies' hardness, with whom they had to fight, sith they were weary with no pains, no more than brute beasts. Caesar's men did daily skirmish hard to the trenches of Pompey's camp, in the which Caesar had ever the

Caesar's dangers and troubles in the Realm of Epirus.

Caesar's army fled from Pompey.

better, saving once only, at what time his men fled with such fear, that all his camp that day was in great hazard to have been cast away. For Pompey came on with his battle upon them, and they were not able to abide it, but were fought with and driven into their camp, and their trenches were filled with dead bodies, which were slain within the very gate and bulwarks of their camp, they were so valiantly pursued. Caesar stood before them that fled, to make them to turn head again : but he could not prevail. For when he would have taken the ensigns to have stayed them, the ensign-bearers threw them down on the ground : so that the enemies took two-and-thirty of them, and Caesar's self also scaped hardly with life. For striking a great big soldier that fled by him, commanding him to stay and turn his face to his enemy, the soldier being afraid lift up his sword to strike at Caesar. But one of Caesar's pages, preventing him, gave him such a blow with his sword, that he strake off his shoulder. Caesar that day was brought unto so great extremity, that (if Pompey had not either for fear or spiteful fortune left off to follow his victory, and retired into his camp, being contented to have driven his enemies into their camp) returning to his camp with his friends, he said unto them : 'The victory this day had been our enemies', if they had had a captain that could have told how to have overcome.' So, when he was come to his lodging, he went to bed, and that night troubled him more than any night that ever he had. For still his

Caesar's words of Pompey's victory.

JULIUS CAESAR

mind ran with great sorrow of the foul fault he had committed in leading of his army, of self-will to remain there so long by the seaside, his enemies being the stronger by sea : considering that he had before him a goodly country, rich and plentiful of all things, and goodly cities of Macedon and Thessaly, and had not the wit to bring the war from thence, but to lose his time in a place, where he was rather besieged of his enemies for lack of victuals, than that he did besiege them by force of arms. Thus fretting and chafing to see himself so straighted with victuals, and to think of his ill luck, he raised his camp, intending to go set upon Scipio, making accompt, that either he should draw Pompey to battle against his will, when he had not the sea at his back to furnish him with plenty of victuals, or else that he should easily overcome Scipio, finding him alone, unless he were aided. This remove of Caesar's camp did much encourage Pompey's army and his captains, who would needs in any case have followed after him, as though he had been overcome, and had fled. But for Pompey himself, he would in no respect hazard battle, which was a matter of so great importance. For finding himself well provided of all things necessary to tarry time, he thought it better to draw this war out in length by tract of time the rather to consume this little strength that remained in Caesar's army : of the which the best men were marvellous well trained and good soldiers, and for valiantness at one day's

Caesar troubled in mind after his loss.

Pompey's determination for the war.

battle were incomparable. But on th' other side again, to remove here and there so oft, and to fortify their camp where they came, and to besiege any wall, or to keep watch all night in their armour: the most part of them could not do it by reason of their age, being then unable to away with that pains, so that the weakness of their bodies did also take away the life and courage of their hearts. Furthermore, there fell a pestilent disease among them, that came by ill meats hunger drave them to eat: yet was not this the worst. For, besides, he had no store of money, neither could tell how to come by victuals: so that it seemed in all likelihood, that in very short time he would come to nothing. For these respects Pompey would in no case fight, and yet had he but Cato only of his mind in that, who stuck in it the rather, because he would avoid shedding of his countrymen's blood. For when Cato had viewed the dead bodies slain in the camp of his enemies, at the last skirmish that was between them, the which were no less than a thousand persons, he covered his face and went away weeping. All other but he contrarily fell out with him, and blamed him, because he so long refrained from battle: and some pricked him forward, and called him Agamemnon, and king of kings, saying that he delayed this war in this sort, because he would not leave his authority to command them all, and that he was glad always to see so many captains round about him, which came to his lodging to honour him, and wait upon him. And Favonius also, a

Pompey called Agamemnon, and king of kings.

JULIUS CAESAR 65

harebrained fellow, franticly counterfeiting the round and plain speech of Cato, made as though he was marvellous angry, and said : 'Is it not great pity that we shall not eat this year of Tusculum figs, and all for Pompey's ambitious mind to reign alone?' And Afranius, who not long before was but lately come out of Spain, (where, because he had but ill success, he was accused of treason, that for money he had sold his army unto Caesar,) he went busily asking, why they fought not with that merchant, unto whom they said he had sold the province of Spain? So that Pompey with these kind of speeches, against his will, was driven to follow Caesar, to fight with him. Then was Caesar at the first marvellously perplexed and troubled by the way: because he found none that would give him any victuals, being despised of every man for the late loss and overthrow he had received. But after that he had taken the city of Gomphi in Thessaly, he did not only meet with plenty of victuals to relieve his army with, but he strangely also did rid them of their disease. For the soldiers, meeting with plenty of wine, drinking hard, and making merry, drave away the infection of the pestilence. For they disposed themselves unto dancing, masking, and playing the Baccherians by the way: insomuch that drinking drunk they overcame their disease, and made their bodies new again. When they both came into the country of Pharsalia, and both camps lay before th' other Pompey returned again to his former determination,

The city of Gomphi in Thessaly.

66 JULIUS CAESAR

and the rather, because he had ill signs and tokens of misfortune in his sleep. For he thought in his sleep that when he entered into the theatre, all the Romans received him with great clapping of hands. Whereupon, they that were about him grew to such boldness and security, assuring themselves of victory, that Domitius, Spinther, and Scipio in a bravery contended between themselves for the chief Bishopric which Caesar had. Furthermore, there were divers that sent unto Rome to hire the nearest houses unto the market-place, as being the fittest places for Praetors and Consuls: making their accompt already, that those officers could not scape them incontinently after the wars. But besides those, the young gentlemen and Roman knights were marvellous desirous to fight, that were bravely mounted, and armed with glistering gilt armours, their horses fat and very finely kept, and themselves goodly young men, to the number of seven thousand, where the gentlemen of Caesar's side were but one thousand only. The number of his footmen also were much after the same reckoning. For he had five-and-forty 'thousand against two-and-twenty thousand. Wherefore Caesar called his soldiers together, and told them how Cornificius was at hand, who brought two whole legions, and that he had fifteen ensigns led by Calenus, the which he made to stay about Megara and Athens. Then he asked them if they would tarry for that aid or not, or whether they

Pompey's dream in Pharsalia.

The security of the Pompeians.

Pompey's army as great again as Caesar's

JULIUS CAESAR

would rather themselves alone venture battle. The soldiers cried out to him, and prayed him not to defer battle, but rather to devise some fetch to make the enemy fight as soon as he could. Then, as he sacrificed unto the gods for the purifying of his army, the first beast was no sooner sacrificed, but his soothsayer assured him that he should fight within three days. Caesar asked him again if he saw in the sacrifices any lucky sign or token of good luck. The soothsayer answered, 'For that thou shalt answer thyself better than I can do: for the gods do promise us a marvellous great change and alteration of things that are now, unto another clean contrary. For if thou beest well now, dost thou think to have worse fortune hereafter? And if thou be ill, assure thyself thou shalt have better.' The night before the battle, as he went about midnight to visit the watch, men saw a great firebrand in the element, all of a light fire, that came over Caesar's camp, and fell down in Pompey's. In the morning also, when they relieved the watch, they heard a false alarm in the enemies' camp, without any apparent cause: which they commonly call a sudden fear, that makes men beside themselves. This notwithstanding, Caesar thought not to fight that day, but was determined to have raised his camp from thence, and to have gone towards the city of Scotusa: and his tents in his camp were already overthrown when his scouts came in with great speed, to bring him news that his enemies were

A wonder seen in the element before the battle of Pharsalia.

preparing themselves to fight. Then he was very glad, and, after he had made his prayers unto the gods to help him that day, he set his men in battle ray, and divided them into three squadrons: giving the middle battle unto Domitius Calvinus, and the left wing unto Antonius, and placed himself in the right wing, choosing his place to fight in the tenth legion. But seeing that against that his enemies had set all their horsemen, he was half afraid when he saw the great number of them and so brave besides. Wherefore he closely made six ensigns to come from the rearward of his battle, whom he had laid as an ambush behind his right wing, having first appointed his soldiers what they should do, when the horsemen of the enemies came to give them charge. On th' other side, Pompey placed himself in the right wing of his battle, gave the left wing unto Domitius, and the middle battle unto Scipio his father-in-law. Now all the Roman knights (as we have told you before) were placed in the left wing of purpose to environ Caesar's right wing behind, and to give their hottest charge there, where the general of their enemies was: making their accompt, that there was no squadron of footmen, how thick soever they were, that could receive the charge of so great a troop of horsemen, and that at the first onset they should overthrow them all and march upon their bellies. When the trumpets on either side did sound the alarum to the battle, Pompey commanded his footmen that they should

Caesar's army and his order of battle in the fields of Pharsalia

Pompey's army and his order of battle.

stand still without stirring, to receive the charge of their enemies, until they came to throwing of their darts. Wherefore Caesar afterwards said that Pompey had committed a foul fault, not to consider that the charge which is given running with fury, besides that it giveth the more strength also unto their blows, doth set men's hearts also a-fire: for the common hurling of all the soldiers that run together is unto them as a box on the ear that sets men a-fire. Then Caesar, making his battle march forward to give the onset, saw one of his captains (a valiant man and very skilful in war, in whom he had also great confidence) speaking to his soldiers that he had under his charge, encouraging them to fight like men that day. So he called him aloud by his name and said unto him: 'Well, Caius Crassinius, what hope shall we have to-day? How are we determined, to fight it out manfully?'" Then Crassinius, casting up his hand, answered him aloud: 'This day, O Caesar, we shall have a noble victory, and I promise thee ere night thou shalt praise me alive or dead.' When he had told him so, he was himself the foremost man that gave charge upon his enemies, with his band following of him, being about sixscore men, and making a lane through the foremost ranks, with great slaughter he entered far into the battle of his enemies: until that, valiantly fighting in this sort, he was thrust in at length in the mouth with a sword, that the point of it came out again at his neck. Now, the footmen

An ill counsel and foul fault of Pompey.

of both battles being come to sword, the horsemen of the left wing of Pompey did march as fiercely also, spreading out their troops, to compass in the right wing of Caesar's battle. But before they began to give charge, the six ensigns of footmen which Caesar had laid in ambush behind him, they began to run full upon them, not throwing away their darts far off as they were wont to do, neither striking their enemies on the thighs nor on the legs, but to seek to hit them full in the eyes, and to hurt them in the face, as Caesar had taught them. For he hoped that these lusty young gentlemen that had not been often in the wars, nor were used to see themselves hurt, and the which being in the prime of their youth and beauty, would be afraid of those hurts, as well for the fear of the present danger to be slain, as also for that their faces should not for ever be deformed. As indeed it came to pass, for they could never abide that they should come so near their faces with the points of their darts, but hung down their heads for fear to be hit with them in their eyes, and turned their backs, covering their face, because they should not be hurt. Then, breaking of themselves, they began at length cowardly to fly, and were occasion also of the loss of all the rest of Pompey's army. For they that had broken them ran immediately to set upon the squadron of the footmen behind, and slew them. Then Pompey, seeing his horsemen from the other wing of his battle so scattered and dispersed flying

The battle in the fields of Pharsalia.

Caesar's stratagem.

Caesar overcometh Pompey.

away, forgat that he was any more Pompey the great which he had been before, but rather was like a man whose wits the gods had taken from him, being afraid and amazed with the slaughter sent from above : and so retired into his tent speaking never a word, and sat there to see the end of this battle. Until at length, all his army being overthrown and put to flight, the enemies came, and got up upon the rampers and defence of his camp, and fought hand to hand with them that stood to defend the same. Then, as a man come to himself again, he spake but this only word : "<u>What, even into our camp</u> ?" So in haste, casting off his coat armour and apparel of a general, he shifted him, and put on such as became his miserable fortune, and so stale out of his camp. Furthermore, what he did after this overthrow, and how he had put himself into the hands of the Egyptians, by whom he was miserably slain, we have set it forth at large in his life. Then Caesar, entering into Pompey's camp, and seeing the bodies laid on the ground that were slain, and others also that were a-killing, said, fetching a great sigh : ' It was their own doing, and against my will.' For Caius Caesar, after he had won so many famous conquests, and overcome so many great battles, had been utterly condemned notwithstanding, if he had departed from his army. Asinius Pollio writeth that he spake these words then in Latin, which he afterwards wrote in Greek, and saith furthermore that the most part of them which were put to the sword in the

Pompey's flight.

camp were slaves and bondmen, and that there were not slain in all at this battle above six thousand soldiers. As for them that were taken prisoners, Caesar did put many of them amongst his legions, and did pardon also many men of estimation, among whom Brutus was one, that afterwards slew Caesar himself: and it is reported that Caesar was very sorry for him, when he could not immediately be found after the battle, and that he rejoiced again, when he knew he was alive, and that he came to yield himself unto him. Caesar had many signs and tokens of victory before this battle: but the notablest of all other that happened to him was in the city of Tralles. For in the temple of victory within the same city there was an image of Caesar, and the earth all about it very hard of itself, and was paved besides with hard stone: and yet some say that sprang up a palm hard by the base of the same image. In the city of Padua, Caius Cornelius, an excellent soothsayer, (a countryman and friend of Titus Livius the historiographer) was by chance at that time set to behold the flying of birds. He (as Livy reporteth) knew the very time when the battle began, and told them that were present, 'Even now they give the onset on both sides, and both armies do meet at this instant.' Then sitting down again to consider of the birds, after he had bethought him of the signs he suddenly rose up on his feet, and cried out as a man possessed with

Brutus, that slew Caesar, taken prisoner at the battle of Pharsalia.

Signs and tokens of Caesar's victory.

A strange tale of Cornelius, an excellent prognosticator.

JULIUS CAESAR

some spirit, 'Oh Caesar, the victory is thine.' Every man wondering to see him, he took the crown he had on his head, and made an oath that he would never put it on again, till the event of his prediction had proved his art true. Livy testifieth that it so came to pass. Caesar afterwards giving freedom unto the Thessalians, in respect of the victory which he won in their country, he followed after Pompey. When he came into Asia, he gave freedom also unto the Gnidians for Theopompus' sake, who had gathered the fables together. He did release Asia also the third part of the tribute which the inhabitants paid unto the Romans. Then he came into Alexandria, after Pompey was slain: and detested Theodotus that presented him Pompey's head, and turned his head at o' side because he would not see it. Notwithstanding, he took his seal and beholding it wept. Furthermore, he courteously used all Pompey's friends and familiars, who wandering up and down the country were taken of the king of Egypt, and won them all to be at his commandment. Continuing these courtesies, he wrote unto his friends at Rome, that the greatest pleasure he took of his victory was, that he daily saved the lives of some of his countrymen that bare arms against him. And, for the war he made in Alexandria, some say he needed not have done it, but that he *willingly did it for the love of Cleopatra:[1] wherein he won

Caesar's clemency in victory.

The cause of Caesar's war in Alexandria.

[1] Cf. *Antony and Cleopatra*, I. v. 29, 30, 66–74.

little honour, and besides did put his person in great danger. Others do lay the fault upon the king of Egypt's ministers, but specially on Pothinus the eunuch, who, bearing the greatest sway of all the king's servants, after he had caused Pompey to be slain and driven Cleopatra from the court, secretly laid wait all the ways he could how he might likewise kill Caesar. Wherefore Caesar, hearing an inkling of it, began thenceforth to spend all the night long in feasting and banqueting, that his person might be in the better safety. But besides all this, Pothinus the eunuch spake many things openly not to be borne, only to shame Caesar and to stir up the people to envy him. For he made his soldiers have the worst and oldest wheat that could be gotten: then, if they did complain of it, he told them they must be contented, seeing they eat at another man's cost. And he would serve them also at the table in treen and earthen dishes, saying that Caesar had away all their gold and silver, for a debt that the king's father (that then reigned) did owe unto him : which was a thousand seven hundred and fifty myriads, whereof Caesar had before forgiven seven hundred and fifty thousand unto his children. Howbeit then he asked a million to pay his soldiers withal. Thereto Pothinus answered him that at that time he should do better to follow his other causes of greater importance, and afterwards that he should at more leisure recover his debt, with the king's good will and favour. Caesar replied unto him and said, that he

JULIUS CAESAR 75

would not ask counsel of the Egyptians for his affairs, but would be paid : and thereupon secretly sent for Cleopatra which was in the country to come unto him. She, only taking Apollodorus Sicilian of all her friends, took a little boat and went away with him in it in the night, and came and landed hard by the *foot of the castle. Then, having no other mean *to come in to the court without being known, she *laid herself down upon a mattress or flock-bed, *which Apollodorus her friend tied and bound up *together like a bundle with a great leather thong, *and so took her up on his back, and brought her *thus hampered in this fardel unto Caesar, in at *the castle gate.¹ This was the first occasion (as it is reported) that made Caesar to love her : but afterwards, when he saw her sweet conversation and pleasant entertainment, he fell then in further liking with her, and did reconcile her again unto her brother the king, with condition that they two jointly should reign together. Upon this new reconciliation a great feast being prepared, a slave of Caesar's that was his barber, the fearfullest wretch that lived, still busily prying and listening abroad in every corner, being mistrustful by nature, found that Pothinus and Achillas did lie in wait to kill his master Caesar. This being proved unto Caesar, he did set such sure watch about the hall where the feast was made, that, in fine, he slew

Cleopatra came to Caesar.

Cleopatra trussed up in a mattress and so brought to Caesar upon Apollodorus' back.

¹ Cf. *Antony and Cleopatra*, II. vi. 68–70.

the eunuch Pothinus himself. Achillas, on th' other side, saved himself and fled unto the king's camp, where he raised a marvellous dangerous and difficult war for Caesar: because, he having then but a few men about him as he had, he was to fight against a great and strong city. The first danger he fell into was for the lack of water he had: for that his enemies had stopped the mouth of the pipes, the which conveyed the water unto the castle. The second danger he had was that seeing his enemies came to take his ships from him, he was driven to repulse that danger with fire, the which burnt the arsenal where the ships lay and that notable library of Alexandria withal. The third danger was in the battle by sea, that was fought by the tower of Phar: where, meaning to help his men that fought by sea, he leapt from the pier into a boat. Then the Egyptians made towards him with their oars on every side: but he, leaping into the sea, with great hazard saved himself by swimming. It is said, that then holding divers books in his hand, he did never let them go, but kept them always upon his head above water, and swam with the other hand, notwithstanding that they shot marvellously at him, and was driven sometime to duck into the water: howbeit the boat was drowned presently. In fine, the king coming to his men that made war with Caesar, he went against him and gave him battle, and won it with great slaughter and effusion of blood. But, for the king, no man could ever

The great library of Alexandria burnt.

Caesar's swimming with books in his hand.

tell what became of him after. Thereupon Caesar made
*Cleopatra his sister Queen of Egypt, who, being
*great with child by him, was shortly brought to bed
*of a son whom the Alexandrians named Caesarion.[1]
From thence he went into Syria, and so going
into Asia, there it was told him that Domitius
was overthrown in battle by Pharnaces the son of
King Mithridates, and was fled out of the realm
of Ponte, with a few men with him: and that this King
Pharnaces, greedily following his victory, was not contented
with the winning of Bithynia and Cappadocia, but further
would needs attempt to win Armenia the less, procuring all
those kings, Princes, and Governors of the provinces thereabouts to rebel against the Romans. Thereupon
Caesar went thither straight with three legions,
and fought a great battle with King Pharnaces by
the city of Zela, where he slew his army and drave him
out of all the realm of Ponte. And because he would
advertise one of his friends of the suddenness of this victory,
he only wrote three words unto Anicius at Rome: *Veni,
Vidi, Vici:* to wit, 'I came, I saw, I overcame.'
These three words, ending all with like sound and
letters in the Latin, have a certain short grace
more pleasant to the ear, than can be well expressed in any other tongue. After this, he returned again
into Italy and came to Rome, ending his year for the

Caesar made Cleopatra Queen of Egypt. Caesarion, Caesar's son, begotten of Cleopatra

Caesar's victory of King Pharnaces

Caesar writeth three words to certify his victory

[1] Cf. *Antony and Cleopatra*, II. ii. 235, 6; III. vi 6.

which he was made Dictator the second time, which office before was never granted for one whole year, but unto him. Then he was chosen Consul for the year following. Afterwards he was very ill spoken of, for that his soldiers in a mutiny having slain two Praetors, Cosconius and Galba, he gave them no other punishment for it, but, instead of calling them soldiers, he named them citizens, and gave unto every one of them a thousand drachmas a man, and great possessions in Italy. He was much misliked also for the desperate parts and madness of Dolabella, for the covetousness of Anicius, for the drunkenness of Antonius and Cornificius, which made Pompey's house be pulled down and builded up again, as a thing not big enough for him, wherewith the Romans were marvellously offended. Caesar knew all this well enough, and would have been contented to have redressed them: but, to bring his matters to pass, he pretended he was driven to serve his turn by such instruments. After the battle of Pharsalia, Cato and Scipio being fled into Africk, King Juba joined with them, and levied a great puissant army. Wherefore Caesar determined to make war with them, and in the midst of winter he took his journey into Sicily. There, because he would take all hope from his Captains and soldiers to make any long abode there, he went and lodged upon the very sands by the seaside, and with the next gale of wind that came he took the sea with three thousand footmen and a few

Caesar's journey into Africk against Cato and Scipio.

horsemen. Then, having put them a-land, unwares to them he hoised sail again, to go fetch the rest of his army, being afraid lest they should meet with some danger in passing over, and meeting them midway he brought them all into his camp. Where, when it was told him that his enemies trusted in an ancient oracle, which said that it was predestined unto the family of the Scipios to be conquerors in Africk: either of purpose to mock Scipio the General of his enemies, or otherwise in good earnest to take the benefit of this name (given by the Oracle) unto himself, in all the skirmishes and battles he fought he gave the charge of his army unto a man of mean quality and accompt, called Scipio Sallution, who came of the race of Scipio African, and made him always his General when he fought. For he was eftsoons compelled to weary and harry his enemies: for that neither his men in his camp had corn enough, nor his beasts forage, but his soldiers were driven to take seaweeds, called *alga*, and (washing away the brackishness thereof with fresh water, putting to it a little herb called dog's-tooth) to cast it so to their horse to eat. For the Numidians (which are light horsemen, and very ready of service), being a great number together, would be on a sudden in every place, and spread all the fields over thereabout, so that no man durst peep out of the camp to go for forage. And one day as the men of arms were staying to behold an African doing notable things in dancing and playing with the flute:

Caesar's troubles in Africk. Alga and dog's-tooth given to the horse to eat.

JULIUS CAESAR

they being set down quietly to take their pleasure of the view thereof, having in the meantime given their slaves their horses to hold, the enemies stealing suddenly upon them compassed them in round about, and slew a number of them in the field, and chasing the other also that fled followed them pell-mell into their camp. Furthermore, had not Caesar himself in person and Asinius Pollio with him, gone out of the camp to the rescue and stayed them that fled, the war that day had been ended. There was also another skirmish where his enemies had the upper hand, in the which it is reported that Caesar, taking the ensign-bearer by the collar that carried the eagle in his hand, stayed him by force, and, turning his face, told him: 'See, there be thy enemies.' These advantages did lift up Scipio's heart aloft, and gave him courage to hazard battle: and, leaving Afranius on the one hand of him, and King Juba on the other hand, both their camps lying near to other, he did fortify himself by the city of Thapsacus, above the lake, to be a safe refuge for them all in this battle. But whilst he was busy intrenching of himself Caesar having marvellous speedily passed through a great country full of wood, by by-paths which men would never have mistrusted, he stale upon some behind, and sudden assailed the other before, so that he overthrew them all, and made them fly. Then following this first good hap he had, he went forthwith to set upon the camp of Afranius, the which he took a

Caesar's dangers in Africk.

Caesar's great victory and small loss

JULIUS CAESAR

the first onset, and the camp of the Numidians also, King Juba being fled. Thus in a little piece of the day only, he took three camps and slew fifty thousand of his enemies, and lost but fifty of his soldiers. In this sort is set down th' effect of this battle by some writers. Yet others do write also, that Caesar self was not there in person at th' execution of this battle. For as he did set his men in battle ray, the falling sickness took him, whereunto he was given, and therefore, feeling it coming, before he was overcome withal, he was carried into a castle not far from thence where the battle was fought, and there took his rest till th' extremity of his disease had left him. Now, for the Praetors and Consuls that scaped from this battle, many of them being taken prisoners did kill themselves, and others also Caesar did put to death : but, he being specially desirous of all men else to have Cato alive in his hands, he went with all possible speed unto the city of Utica, whereof Cato was Governor, by means whereof he was not at the battle. Notwithstanding, being certified by the way that Cato had slain himself with his own hands, he then made open shew that he was very sorry for it, but why or wherefore no man could tell. But this is true, that Caesar said at that present time : 'O Cato, I envy thy death, because thou didst envy my glory to save thy life.' This notwithstanding, the book that he wrote afterwards against Cato being dead did shew no very great affection nor pitiful heart

Caesar troubled with the falling sickness.

Caesar was sorry for the death of Cato.

towards him. For how could he have pardoned him, if living he had had him in his hands, that being dead did speak so vehemently against him? Notwithstanding, men suppose he would have pardoned him, if he had taken him alive, by the clemency he shewed unto Cicero, Brutus, and divers others that had borne arms against him. Some report that he wrote that book, not so much for any private malice he had to his death, as for a civil ambition, upon this occasion: Cicero had written a book in praise of Cato, which he entitled *Cato*. This book in likelihood was very well liked of, by reason of the eloquence of the orator that made it, and of the excellent subject thereof. Caesar therewith was marvellously offended, thinking that to praise him of whose death he was author was even as much as to accuse himself: and therefore he wrote a letter against him, and heaped up a number of accusations against Cato, and entitled the book *Anticaton*. Both these books have favourers unto this day, some defending the one for the love they bare to Caesar, and others allowing the other for Cato's sake. Caesar, being now returned out of Africk, first of all made an oration to the people, wherein he greatly praised and commended this his last victory, declaring unto them that he had conquered so many countries unto the Empire of Rome, that he could furnish the commonwealth yearly with two hundred thousand bushels of wheat, and twenty hundred thousand pound

Caesar wrote against Cato being dead.

Cicero wrote a book in praise of Cato being dead.

JULIUS CAESAR

weight of oil. Then he made three triumphs, the one for Egypt, the other for the kingdom of Ponte, and the third for Africk: not because he had overcome Scipio there, but King Juba. Whose son being likewise called Juba, being then a young boy, was led captive in the show of this triumph. But this his imprisonment fell out happily for him : for, where he was but a barbarous Numidian, by the study he fell unto when he was prisoner he came afterwards to be reckoned one of the wisest historiographers of the Grecians.

Juba, the son of King Juba, a famous historiographer.

After these three triumphs ended, he very liberally rewarded his soldiers : and to curry favour with the people, he made great feasts and common sports. For he feasted all the Romans at one time at two-and-twenty thousand tables, and gave them the pleasure to see divers sword-players to fight at the sharp, and battles also by sea, for the remembrance of his daughter Julia, which was dead long before. Then, after all these sports, he made the people (as the manner was) to be mustered : and, where there were at the last musters before three hundred and twenty thousand citizens, at this muster only there were but a hundred and fifty thousand. Such misery and destruction had this civil war brought unto the commonwealth of Rome, and had consumed such a number of Romans, not speaking at all of the mischiefs and calamities it had brought unto all the rest of Italy, and to the other provinces per-

Caesar's feasting of the Romans.

The muster taken of the Romans.

taining to Rome. After all these things were ended, he
was chosen Consul the fourth time, and went into
Spain to make war with the sons of Pompey
who were yet but very young, but had notwithstanding raised a marvellous great army together, and
shewed to have had manhood and courage worthy to command such an army, insomuch as they put Caesar himself
in great danger of his life. The greatest battle
that was fought between them in all this war was
by the city of Munda. For then Caesar seeing his
men sorely distressed, and having their hands full
of their enemies: he ran into the press among
his men that fought, and cried out unto them: 'What are
ye not ashamed to be beaten and taken prisoners, yielding
yourselves with your own hands to these young boys?'
And so, with all the force he could make, having
with much ado put his enemies to flight, he slew
above thirty thousand of them in the field, and
lost of his own men a thousand of the best he had. After
this battle he went into his tent, and told his friends that
he had often before fought for victory, but this last time
now that he had fought for the safety of his own life. He
won this battle on the very feast day of the Bacchanalians,
in the which men say that Pompey the Great went out of
Rome about four years before, to begin this civil war. For
his sons, the younger scaped from the battle: but within
few days after Didius brought the head of the elder. This

Caesar Consul the fourth time

Battle fought betwixt Caesar and the young Pompeys by the city of Munda.

Caesar's victory of the sons of Pompey.

JULIUS CAESAR

was the last war that Caesar made. But the triumph he made into Rome for the same did as much offend the Romans, and more, than anything that ever he *had done before : because he had not overcome *Captains that were strangers, nor barbarous kings, but had *destroyed the sons of the noblest man in Rome, whom *fortune had overthrown. And because he had plucked up *his race by the roots, men did not think it meet for him to *triumph so for the calamities of his country, rejoicing at a *thing for the which he had but one excuse to allege in his *defence unto the gods and men, that he was compelled to *do that he did.[1] And the rather they thought it not meet, because he had never before sent letters nor messengers unto the commonwealth at Rome for any victory that he had ever won in all the civil wars : but did always for shame refuse the glory of it. This notwithstanding, the Romans inclining to Caesar's prosperity and taking the bit in the mouth, supposing that, to be ruled by one man alone, it would be a good mean for them to take breath a little, after so many troubles and miseries as they had abidden in these civil wars : they chose him perpetual Dictator. This was a plain tyranny : for to this absolute power of Dictator they added this, never to be afraid to be deposed / Cicero propounded before the Senate, that they should give him such honours as were meet for a man : howbeit others afterwards added-to honours beyond

Caesar's triumph of Pompey's sons.

Caesar Dictator, perpetual.

[1] Cf. *Julius Caesar*, I. i 36-55.

all reason. For, men striving who should most honour him, they made him hateful and troublesome to themselves that most favoured him by reason of the unmeasurable greatness and honours which they gave him. Thereupon, it is reported that even they that most hated him were no less favourers and furtherers of his honours than they that most flattered him: because they might have greater occasions to rise, and that it might appear they had just cause and colour to attempt that they did against him. And now for himself, after he had ended his civil wars, he did so honourably behave himself, that there was no fault to be found in him: and therefore methinks, amongst other honours they gave him, he rightly deserved this, that they should build him a temple of clemency, to thank him for his courtesy he had used unto them in his victory. For he pardoned many of them that had borne arms against him, and furthermore, did prefer some of them to honour and office in the commonwealth: as, amongst others, Cassius and Brutus, both the which were made Praetors. And where Pompey's images had been thrown down, he caused them to be set up again: whereupon Cicero said then, that Caesar setting up Pompey's images again he made his own stand the surer. And when some of his friends did counsel him to have a guard for the safety of his person, and some also did offer themselves to serve him, he would never consent to it, but said, it was*

Marginalia:
The temple of clemency, dedicated unto Caesar for his courtesy

Cassius and Brutus Praetors

Caesar's saying of death

*better to die once, than always to be afraid of death.¹ But to win himself the love and good will of the people, as the honourablest guard and best safety he could have, he made common feasts again, and general distributions of corn. Furthermore, to gratify the soldiers also, he replenished many cities again with inhabitants, which before had been destroyed, and placed them there that had no place to repair unto of the which the noblest and chiefest cities were these two, Carthage and Corinth, and it chanced also that, like as aforetime they had been both taken and destroyed together, even so were they both set afoot again and replenished with people at one self time. And as for great personages, he wan them also, promising some of them to make them Praetors and Consuls in time to come, and unto others honours and preferments, but to all men generally good hope, seeking all the ways he could to make every man contented with his reign. Insomuch as one of the Consuls called Maximus chancing to die a day before his Consulship ended, he declared Caninius Rebilius Consul only for the day that remained. So, divers going to his house (as the manner was) to salute him, and to congratulate with him of his calling and preferment, being newly chosen officer, Cicero pleasantly said, 'Come, let us make haste, and be gone thither before his Consulship come out.' Furthermore, Caesar being born to attempt all

Good will of subjects the best guard and safety for Princes.

Caninius Rebilius Consul for one day.

¹ Cf. *Julius Caesar*, II. ii. 32, 33.

great enterprises, and having an ambitious desire besides to covet great honours, the prosperous good success he had of his former conquests bred no desire in him quietly to enjoy the fruits of his labours, but rather gave him hope of things to come, still kindling more and more in him thoughts of greater enterprises, and desire of new glory, as if that which he had present were stale and nothing worth. This humour of his was no other but an emulation with himself as with another man, and a certain contention to overcome the things he prepared to attempt. For he was determined, and made preparation also, to make war with the Persians. Then, when he had overcome them, to pass through Hyrcania (compassing in the sea Caspium and Mount Caucasus) into the realm of Pontus, and so to invade Scythia: and over-running all the countries and people adjoining unto high Germany, and Germany itself, at length to return by Gaul into Italy, and so to enlarge the Roman Empire round, that it might be every way compassed in with the great sea Oceanus. But whilst he was preparing for this voyage, he attempted to cut the bar of the strait of Peloponnesus, in the place where the city of Corinth standeth. Then he was minded to bring the rivers of Anien and Tiber straight from Rome unto the city of Circeii with a deep channel and high banks cast up on either side, and so to fall into the sea at Terracina, for the better safety and commodity of the merchants that came to Rome to traffic there. Furthermore, he determined

<small>Anien
Tiber, flu.</small>

JULIUS CAESAR

to drain and seaw all the water of the marishes betwixt the cities of Nomentum and Setium, to make it firm land for the benefit of many thousands of people : and on the seacoast next unto Rome to cast great high banks, and to cleanse all the haven about Ostia of rocks and stones hidden under the water, and to take away all other impediments that made the harbourough dangerous for ships, and to make new havens and arsenals meet to harbour such ships as did continually traffic thither. All these things were purposed to be done, but took no effect. But the ordinance of the calendar and reformation of the year, to take away all confusion of time, being exactly calculated by the Mathematicians and brought to perfection, was a great commodity unto all men. *Caesar reformed the inequality of the year.* For the Romans, using then the ancient computation of the year, had not only such incertainty and alteration of the month and times, that the sacrifices and yearly feasts came by little and little to seasons contrary for the purpose they were ordained : but also in the revolution of the sun (which is called *Annus Solaris*) no other nation agreed with them in account : and, of the Romans themselves, only the priests understood it. And therefore, when they listed, they suddenly (no man being able to control them) did thrust in a month above their ordinary number, which they called in old time,[a] *Mercedonius*. Some say that Numa Pompilius was the first that devised this way, to put a month between : but it

[a] *Mercedonius, mensis intercalaris.*

was a weak remedy, and did little help the correction of the errors that were made in the account of the year, to frame them to perfection. But Caesar, committing this matter unto the Philosophers and best expert Mathematicians at that time, did set forth an excellent and perfect calendar, more exactly calculated than any other that was before: the which the Romans do use until this present day, and do nothing err as others in the difference of time. But his enemies notwithstanding that envied his greatness did not stick to find fault withal. As Cicero the Orator, when one said, 'To-morrow the star Lyra will rise:' 'Yea,' said he, 'at the commandment of Caesar,' as if men were compelled so to say and think by Caesar's edict. But the chiefest cause that made him mortally hated was the covetous desire he had to be called king: which first gave the people just cause and next his secret enemies honest colour, to bear him ill will. This notwithstanding, they that procured him this honour and dignity gave it out among the people, that it was written in the Sibylline prophecies, how the Romans might overcome the Parthians, if they made war with them and were led by a king, but otherwise that they were unconquerable. And furthermore they were so bold besides, that, Caesar returning to Rome from the city of Alba, when they came to salute him, they called him king. But the people being offended and Caesar also angry, he said he was not called king, but Caesar. Then, every man keeping silence, he went his way

Why Caesar was hated.

JULIUS CAESAR

heavy and sorrowful. When they had decreed divers honours for him in the Senate, the Consuls and Praetors accompanied with the whole assembly of the Senate went unto him in the market place, where he was set by the pulpit for orations, to tell him what honours they had decreed for him in his absence. But he, sitting still in his majesty, disdaining to rise up unto them when they came in, as if they had been private men, answered them : that his honours had more need to be cut off than enlarged. This did not only offend the Senate, but the common people also, to see that he should so lightly esteem of the Magistrates of the commonwealth : insomuch as every man that might lawfully go his way departed thence very sorrowfully. Thereupon also Caesar rising departed home to his house, and
*tearing open his doublet collar, making his neck bare, he
*cried out aloud to his friends, that his throat was ready to
*offer to any man that would come and cut it.[1] Notwithstanding, it is reported that afterwards, to excuse this folly, he imputed it to his disease, saying, that their wits are not
*perfect which have his disease of the falling evil, when
*standing of their feet they speak to the common people, but
*are soon troubled with a trembling of their body, and a
*sudden dimness and giddiness.[2] But that was not true. For he would have risen up to the Senate, but Cornelius Balbus one of his friends (but rather a flatterer) would not let him,

[1] Cf. *Julius Caesar*, I. ii. 268, 9 ; *Life of Antonius*, Vol. II. p. 19.
[2] *Ibid.* I. ii. 248-58 ; and *ante*, pp. 26, 81.

saying: 'What, do you not remember that you are Caesar and will you not let them reverence you, and do their duties?' Besides these occasions and offences there followed also his shame and reproach, abusing the Tribunes of the people in this sort. At that time the feast Lupercalia[1] was celebrated, the which in old time men say was the feast of shepherds, or herdmen, and is much like unto the feast of the Lycaeans in Arcadia. But howsoever it is, that day there are divers noblemen's sons, young men, (and some of them Magistrates themselves that govern then) which run naked through the city, striking in sport them they meet in their way with leather thongs, hair and all on, to make them give place. And many noblewomen and gentlewomen also go of purpose to stand in their way, and do put forth their hands to be striken, as scholars hold them out to their schoolmaster to be striken with the ferula: persuading themselves that, being with child, they shall have good delivery, and also, being barren, that it will make them to conceive with child.

The feast Lupercalia

Antonius, being Consul, was one of the Lupercalians

Caesar sat to behold that sport upon the pulpit for orations, in a chair of gold, apparelled in triumphing manner. Antonius, who was Consul at that time, was one of them that ran this holy course.[2] So, when he came into the marketplace, the people made a lane for him to run at liberty, and he

[1] Cf. *Julius Caesar*, I. i. 71.
[2] *Ibid.* I. ii. 3-9, *Life of Antonius*, Vol. II pp. 18, 19.

JULIUS CAESAR 93

*came to Caesar, and presented him a Diadem wreathed
*about with laurel. Whereupon there rose a certain cry of
*rejoicing, not very great, done only by a few appointed for
*the purpose. But when Caesar refused the
*Diadem, then all the people together made an out-
*cry of joy. Then, Antonius offering it him again,
*there was a second shout of joy, but yet of a
*few. But when Caesar refused it again the second time,
*then all the whole people shouted.[1] Caesar having made this
proof found that the people did not like of it, and thereupon
rose out of his chair, and commanded the crown to be carried
*unto Jupiter in the Capitol. After that, there were set up
*image of Caesar in the city with Diadems upon their heads,
*like kings. Those the two Tribunes, Flavius and Marullus,
*went and pulled down:[2] and furthermore, meeting with
them that first saluted Caesar as king, they committed them
to prison. The people followed them rejoicing at it, and
called them Brutes, because of Brutus, who had in old time
driven the kings out of Rome, and that brought the kingdom
of one person unto the government of the Senate and
*people. Caesar was so offended withal, that he deprived
*Marullus and Flavius of their Tribuneships,[3] and, accusing
them, he spake also against the people, and called them
Bruti and *Cumani*, to wit, beasts and fools. Hereupon the

<small>Antonius presented the Diadem to Caesar.</small>

---

[1] Cf. *Julius Caesar*, I. ii. 219-246; *Life of Antonius*, Vol. II. p. 19.

[2] *Ibid.* I. i. 68-73; *Life of Brutus*, p. 121.

[3] *Ibid.* I. ii. 289-91; *Life of Antonius*, Vol. II. p. 20.

people went straight unto Marcus Brutus, who from his father came of the first Brutus and by his mother of the house of the Servilians, a noble house as any was in Rome, and was also nephew and son-in-law of Marcus Cato. Notwithstanding, the great honours and favour Caesar shewed unto him kept him back, that of himself alone he did not conspire nor consent to depose him of his kingdom. For

<small>Caesar saved Marcus Brutus' life after the battle of Pharsalia.</small> Caesar did not only save his life after the battle of Pharsalia when Pompey fled, and did at his request also save many more of his friends besides: but, furthermore, he put a marvellous confidence in him. For he had already preferred him to the Praetorship for that year, and furthermore was appointed to be Consul the fourth year after that, having through Caesar's friendship obtained it before Cassius, who likewise made suit for the same: and Caesar also, as it is reported, said in this contention, 'Indeed Cassius hath alleged best reason, but yet shall he not be chosen before Brutus.'

<small>Brutus conspireth against Caesar.</small> Some one day accusing Brutus while he practised this conspiracy, Caesar would not hear of it, but clapping his hand on his body, told them, 'Brutus will look for this skin:' meaning thereby that Brutus for his virtue deserved to rule after him, but yet that for ambition's sake he would not shew himself unthankful nor dishonourable. Now they that desired change and* wished Brutus only their Prince and Governor above* all other, they durst not come to him themselves to tell*

JULIUS CAESAR

*him what they would have him to do, but in the night
*did cast sundry papers into the Praetor's seat where he
*gave audience, and the most of them to this effect : ' Thou
—*sleepest, Brutus, and art not Brutus indeed.'[1] Cassius,
finding Brutus' ambition stirred up the more by
these seditious bills, did prick him forward and
egg him on the more for a private quarrel he had
conceived against Caesar : the circumstance where-
*of we have set down more at large in Brutus' life. Caesar

<small>Cassius stirreth up Brutus against Caesar.</small>

*also had Cassius in great jealousy and suspected him much :
*whereupon he said on a time to his friends, ' What will
*Cassius do, think ye ? I like not his pale looks.' Another
*time, when Caesar's friends complained unto him of
*Antonius and Dolabella, that they pretended some mischief
*towards him : he answered them again, ' As for those fat
*men and smooth-combed heads,' quoth he, ' I never reckon
*of them : but these pale-visaged and carrion lean people, I
*fear them most :' meaning Brutus and Cassius.[2] Certainly,
destiny may easier be foreseen than avoided : con-
*sidering the strange and wonderful signs that were
*said to be seen before Caesar's death. For, touch-
*ing the fires in the element and spirits running

<small>Predictions and foreshews of Caesar's death.</small>

*up and down in the night, and also the solitary birds to be
*seen at noon-days sitting in the great market place: are not

---

[1] Cf. *Julius Caesar*, I. iii. 140-44, II. i. 46 ; *Life of Brutus*, pp 120, 121.

[2] Cf. *Julius Caesar*, I. ii. 191-200 ; *Life of Brutus*, p. 119 ; *Life of Antonius*, Vol. II. p. 18.

all these signs perhaps worth the noting in such a wonderful* chance as happened?[1] But Strabo the Philosopher writeth* that divers men were seen going up and down in fire:[2]* and furthermore, that there was a slave of the soldiers, that* did cast a marvellous burning flame out of his hand, inso-* much as they that saw it thought he had been burnt, but* when the fire was out, it was found he had no hurt.[3]* Caesar self also, doing sacrifice unto the gods, found that* one of the beasts which was sacrificed had no heart:[4] and* that was a strange thing in nature, how a beast could live without a heart. Furthermore, there was a certain* Soothsayer that had given Caesar warning long* time afore, to take heed of the day of the Ides of* March (which is the fifteenth of the month), for* on that day he should be in great danger. That* day being come, Caesar going unto the Senate-house, and* speaking merrily to the Soothsayer, told him, 'The Ides of† March be come:' 'So be they,' softly answered the Sooth-† sayer, 'but yet are they not past.'[5] And the very day† before, Caesar, supping with Marcus Lepidus, sealed certain letters, as he was wont to do, at the board: so, talk falling out amongst them, reasoning what death was best, he preventing their opinions cried out aloud, 'Death unlooked for.' Then going to bed the same night as his manner was,

Caesar's day of his death prognosticated by a Soothsayer.

---

[1] Cf. *Julius Caesar*, I. iii. 10, 25–32.
[2] *Ibid.* I. iii. 25; II. ii. 19.
[3] *Ibid.* I. iii. 15–18.
[4] *Ibid.* II. ii. 37–40.
[5] *Ibid.* III. i. 1, 2

JULIUS CAESAR

*and lying with his wife Calpurnia, all the windows and
*doors of his chamber flying open, the noise awoke him, and
*made him afraid when he saw such light : but more, when
*he heard his wife Calpurnia, being fast asleep, weep and
*sigh, and put forth many fumbling lamentable speeches.
*For she dreamed that Caesar was slain,[1] and that
she had him in her arms. Others also do deny
that she had any such dream, as amongst other
Titus Livius writeth, that it was in this sort. The
Senate having set upon the top of Caesar's house, for an
ornament and setting forth of the same, a certain pinnacle,
Calpurnia dreamed that she saw it broken down, and that
*she thought she lamented and wept for it. Insomuch that,
*Caesar rising in the morning, she prayed him if it were
*possible not to go out of the doors that day,[2] but to adjourn
the session of the Senate until another day. And if that
*he made no reckoning of her dream, yet that he would
*search further of the Soothsayers by their sacrifices, to know
*what should happen him that day.[3] Thereby it seemed that
Caesar likewise did fear and suspect somewhat, because his
*wife Calpurnia until that time was never given to any fear
*or superstition :[4] and then, for that he saw her so troubled
in mind with this dream she had. But much more afterwards, when the Soothsayers, having sacrificed many beasts
*one after another, told him that none did like them : then

The dream of Calpurnia Caesar's wife.

---

[1] Cf. *Julius Caesar*, II. ii. 1–3. [2] *Ibid*. II. ii. 76–82.
[3] *Ibid*. II. ii 5, 6. [4] *Ibid*. II. ii. 13, 14.

JULIUS CAESAR

he determined to send Antonius to adjourn the session of the
Senate.[1] But in the meantime came Decius Brutus,
surnamed Albinus, in whom Caesar put such confidence, that in his last will and testament he had
appointed him to be his next heir, and yet was of
the conspiracy with Cassius and Brutus: he, fearing that if
Caesar did adjourn the session that day the conspiracy would
out, laughed the Soothsayers to scorn, and reproved Caesar,
saying: that he gave the Senate occasion to mislike with
him, and that they might think he mocked them, considering that by his commandment they were assembled, and
that they were ready willingly to grant him all things, and
to proclaim him king of all the provinces of the Empire of
Rome out of Italy, and that he should wear his Diadem in
all other places both by sea and land. And furthermore,
that if any man should tell them from him they should
depart for that present time, and return again when
Calpurnia should have better dreams: what would his
enemies and illwillers say, and how could they like of his
friends' words?[2] And who could persuade them otherwise,
but that they would think his dominion a slavery
unto them, and tyrannical in himself? 'And
yet, if it be so,' said he, 'that you utterly mislike
of this day, it is better that you go yourself in
person, and saluting the Senate to dismiss them
till another time.' Therewithal he took Caesar by the

Decius Brutus Albinus' persuasion to Caesar.

Decius Brutus brought Caesar into the senate-house.

[1] Cf. *Julius Caesar*, II. ii. 52-6.   [2] *Ibid.* II. ii. 93-9.

JULIUS CAESAR

hand, and brought him out of his house. Caesar was not gone far from his house, but a bondman, a stranger, did what he could to speak with him : and, when he saw he was put back by the great press and multitude of people that followed him, he went straight unto his house, and put himself into Calpurnia's hands to be kept till Caesar came back again, telling her that he had great matters to
*impart unto him. And one Artemidorus also, born in the
*Isle of Gnidos, a Doctor of Rhetoric in the Greek
*tongue, who by means of his profession was very
*familiar with certain of Brutus' confederates, and
*therefore knew the most part of all their practices

The tokens of the conspiracy against Caesar.

*against Caesar, came and brought him a little bill written
*with his own hand, of all that he meant to tell him. He,
*marking how Caesar received all the supplications that were
*offered him, and that he gave them straight to his men that
*were about him, pressed nearer to him, and said : 'Caesar
*read this memorial to yourself, and that quickly, for they
*be matters of great weight, and touch you nearly.' Caesar,
*took it of him, but could never read it, though he many
*times attempted it, for the number of people that did salute
*him : but holding it still in his hand, keeping it to himself,
*went on withal into the Senate-house.[1] Howbeit other are of opinion that it was some man else that gave him that memorial, and not Artemidorus, who did what he could all the way as he went to give it Caesar, but he was always

[1] Cf. *Julius Caesar*, II. iii , III. i. 3, 6-12.

JULIUS CAESAR

repulsed by the people. For these things they may seem to come by chance: but the place where the murther was prepared, and where the Senate were assembled, and where also there stood up an image of Pompey dedicated by himself amongst other ornaments which he gave unto the Theatre: all these were manifest proofs that it was the ordinance of some god, that made this treason to be executed specially in that very place. It is also reported, that Cassius (though otherwise he did favour the doctrine of* Epicurus)[1] beholding the image of Pompey, before they* entered into the action of their traitorous enterprise, he did softly call upon it to aid him. But the instant danger of the present time, taking away his former reason, did suddenly put him into a furious passion, and made him like a man half beside himself. Now* Antonius, that was a faithful friend to Caesar,* and a valiant man besides of his hands, him* Decius Brutus Albinus entertained out of the Senate house,* having begun a long tale of set purpose.[2] So, Caesar* coming into the house, all the Senate stood up on their feet to do him honour. Then part of Brutus' company and* confederates stood round about Caesar's chair, and part of* them also came towards him, as though they made suit with* Metellus Cimber, to call home his brother again from*

The place where Caesar was slain.

Antonius Caesar's faithful friend.

---

[1] Cf. *Julius Caesar*, V. i. 77, 8.
[2] Cf. *Julius Caesar*, III. i. 25, 6; *Life of Brutus*, p. 164; *Life of Antonius*, Vol. II. pp. 20, 21.

JULIUS CAESAR

*banishment : and thus, prosecuting still their suit, they
*followed Caesar, till he was set in his chair. Who denying
*their petitions, and being offended with them one after
*another, because the more they were denied, the more they
*pressed upon him, and were the earnester with him : [1]
Metellus at length, taking his gown with both his hands,
pulled it over his neck, which was the sign given the con-
*federates to set upon him. Then Casca behind
*him strake him in the neck with his sword : [2]   Casca the first that strake at Caesar.
howbeit the wound was not great nor mortal,
because, it seemed, the fear of such a devilish
attempt did amaze him, and take his strength from him, that
he killed him not at the first blow. But Caesar, turning
straight unto him, caught hold of his sword, and held it
hard : and they both cried out, Caesar in Latin : ' O vile
traitor Casca, what doest thou ? ' And Casca in Greek to
his brother, ' Brother, help me.' At the beginning of this
stir, they that were present, not knowing of the conspiracy,
were so amazed with the horrible sight they saw, that they
had no power to fly, neither to help him, not so much as
once to make any outcry. They on th' other side that had
conspired his death compassed him in on every side with
their swords drawn in their hands, that Caesar turned him
nowhere but he was stricken at by some, and still had naked
*swords in his face, and was hacked and mangled among

---

[1] Cf. *Julius Caesar*, III. 1. 27–75.
[2] *Ibid.* III. 1. 76 ; V. 1. 43, 4.

them, as a wild beast taken of hunters.¹ For it was agreed*
among them that every man should give him a wound,
because all their parts should be in this murther : and then
Brutus himself gave him one wound about his privities.
Men report also that Caesar did still defend himself against
the rest, running every way with his body : but when he*
saw Brutus with his sword drawn in his hand, then he*
pulled his gown over his head, and made no more resistance,²*
and was driven either casually or purposedly by the counsel*
of the conspirators against the base whereupon Pompey's*
image stood, which ran all of a gore-blood till he was*
slain.³ Thus it seemed that the image took just revenge of*
Pompey's enemy, being thrown down on the ground at his
feet, and yielding up his ghost there for the number of
wounds he had upon him. For it is reported that he had*

<small>Caesar slain and had 23 wounds upon him</small> three-and-twenty wounds upon his body :⁴ and*
divers of the conspirators did hurt themselves,
striking one body with so many blows. When
Caesar was slain, the Senate (though Brutus stood*
in the midst amongst them, as though he would have said*
somewhat touching this fact,⁵) presently ran out of the*
house, and flying filled all the city with marvellous fear and
tumult. Insomuch as some did shut-to their doors, others
forsook their shops and warehouses, and others ran to the

---

¹ Cf *Julius Caesar*, III. i. 204–10.
² *Ibid.* III. i. 77 ; ii. 189–92. ³ *Ibid.* III. i. 115 ; ii. 193, 4.
⁴ *Ibid.* V. i. 53. ⁵ *Ibid.* III. i. 82, 3.

JULIUS CAESAR

place to see what the matter was: and others also that had seen it ran home to their houses again. But Antonius and Lepidus, which were two of Caesar's chiefest friends, secretly conveying themselves away, fled into other men's houses, and forsook their own. Brutus and his confederates on th' other side, being yet hot with this murther they had committed, having their swords drawn in their hands, came all in a troop together out of the Senate, and went into the market-place, not as men that made countenance to fly, but otherwise boldly holding up their heads like men of courage, and called to the people to defend their liberty, and stayed to speak with every great personage whom they met in their way. Of them some followed this troop and went amongst them as if they had been of the conspiracy, and falsely challenged part of the honour with them: among them was Caius Octavius, and Lentulus Spinther. But both of them were afterwards put to death, for their vain covetousness of honour, by Antonius and Octavius Caesar the younger: and yet had no part of that honour for the which they were put to death, neither did any man believe that they were any of the confederates, or of counsel with them. For they that did put them to death took revenge rather of the will they had to offend, than of any fact they had committed. The next morning Brutus and his confederates came into the market-place to speak unto the people, who gave them such audience, that it seemed they

The murtherers of Caesar do go to the market-place.

JULIUS CAESAR

neither greatly reproved nor allowed the fact : for by their great silence they showed that they were sorry for Caesar's death, and also that they did reverence Brutus. Now the Senate granted general pardon for all that was past, and to pacify every man, ordained besides that Caesar's funerals should be honoured as a god, and established all things that he had done : and gave certain provinces also and convenient honours unto Brutus and his confederates, whereby every man thought all things were brought to good peace and quietness again. But when they had opened* Caesar's testament, and found a liberal legacy of money* bequeathed unto every citizen of Rome,[1] and that they saw* his body (which was brought into the market place) all bemangled with gashes of swords : then there was no order* to keep the multitude and common people quiet, but they* plucked up forms, tables, and stools, and laid them all about* the body, and setting them afire burnt the corse. Then,* when the fire was well kindled, they took the firebrands,* and went unto their houses that had slain Caesar, to set* them afire.[2] Other also ran up and down the city to see* if they could meet with any of them, to cut them in pieces : howbeit they could meet with never a man of them, because they had locked themselves up safely in their houses. There*

_{Caesar's funerals.}

---

[1] Cf. *Julius Caesar*, III. ii. 134-164, 242-256 ; *Life of Brutus*, p. 137 ; *Life of Antonius*, Vol. II. pp. 23, 24.

[2] Cf. *Julius Caesar*, III. ii. 258-64 ; *Life of Brutus*, p. 137, 8 ; *Life of Antonius*, Vol. II. p. 22.

JULIUS CAESAR

*was one of Caesar's friends called Cinna, that had a
*marvellous strange and terrible dream the night
*before. He dreamed that Caesar bade him to *Cinna's dream of Caesar.*
*supper, and that he refused, and would not go:
*then that Caesar took him by the hand, and led him against
*his will. Now Cinna hearing at that time that they burnt
*Caesar's body in the market place, notwithstanding that
*he feared his dream and had an ague on him besides, he
*went into the market place to honour his funerals. When
*he came thither, one of mean sort asked him what his name
*was? He was straight called by his name. The first man
*told it to another, and that other unto another, so that it
*ran straight through them all, that he was one of them that
*murdered Caesar (for indeed one of the traitors to Caesar
*was also called Cinna as himself): wherefore,
*taking him for Cinna the murderer, they fell upon *The murther of Cinna.*
*him with such fury, that they presently dispatched
*him in the market place.[1] This stir and fury made Brutus
and Cassius more afraid than of all that was past, and
therefore, within few days after, they departed out of
Rome: and touching their doings afterwards, and what
calamity they suffered till their deaths, we have written it
at large in the life of Brutus. Caesar died at six- *Caesar 56*
and-fifty years of age: and Pompey also lived not *year old at his*
passing four years more than he. So he reaped *death.*
no other fruit of all his reign and dominion, which he had

[1] Cf. *Julius Caesar*, III. iii.; *Life of Brutus*, pp. 138, 9.

so vehemently desired all his life, and pursued with such extreme danger, but a vain name only, and a superficial glory that procured him the envy and hatred of his country. But his great prosperity and good fortune, that favoured him all his lifetime, did continue afterwards in the revenge of his death, pursuing the murtherers both by sea and land, till they had not left a man more to be executed, of all them that were actors or counsellors in the conspiracy of his death. Furthermore, of all the chances that happen unto men upon the earth, that which came to Cassius above all other is most to be wondered at. For he, being overcome in battle at the journey of* Philippi, slew himself with the same sword with* the which he strake Caesar.[1] Again, of signs in* the element, the great comet, which seven nights together was seen very bright after Caesar's death, the eight night after was never seen more. Also the brightness of the sun was darkened, the which all that year through rose very pale, and shined not out, whereby it gave but small heat: therefore the air being very cloudy and dark, by the weakness of the heat that could not come forth, did cause the earth to bring forth but raw and unripe fruit, which rotted before it could ripe. But, above all, the ghost that appeared unto Brutus shewed plainly that the gods were offended with the murther

The revenge of Caesar's death.

Cassius being overthrown at the battle of Philippi slew himself with the self-same sword wherewith he strake Caesar.

Wonders seen in the element after Caesar's death. A great Comet.

---

[1] Cf. *Julius Caesar*, V. iii. 41-6.

JULIUS CAESAR

*of Caesar. The vision was thus. Brutus, being ready to pass
*over his army from the city of Abydos to the other coast
*lying directly against it, slept every night (as his manner was)
*in his tent, and being yet awake thinking of his affairs, (for
*by report he was as careful a Captain, and lived with as
*little sleep, as ever man did,) he thought he heard a noise
*at his tent door, and, looking towards the light of   Brutus'
*the lamp that waxed very dim, he saw a horrible vision
*vision of a man, of a wonderful greatness, and dreadful
*look, which at the first made him marvellously afraid
*But when he saw that it did him no hurt, but stood by his
*bedside and said nothing, at length he asked him what
the was. The image answered him : 'I am thy   A spirit
†ill angel, Brutus, and thou shalt see me by the appeared
†city of Philippi.' Then Brutus replied again,   Brutus.
†and said . 'Well, I shall see thee then.' Therewithal
*the spirit presently vanished from him.[1] After that time
Brutus being in battle near unto the city of Philippi against
Antonius and Octavius Caesar, at the first battle he won
the victory, and, overthrowing all them that with- The
stood him, he drave them into young Caesar's   second
*camp, which he took. The second battle being at of the
*hand, this spirit appeared again unto him, but spake Brutus.
*never a word. Thereupon Brutus, knowing he should die,[2]

[1] Cf. *Julius Caesar*, IV. iii. 274-84 ; *Life of Brutus*, p. 163.
[2] Cf. *Julius Caesar*, V. v. 19, 20 ; *Life of Brutus*, p. 183 ; *Antony and Cleopatra*, II. vi. 12, 13.

did put himself to all hazard in battle, but yet fighting could not be slain. So, seeing his men put to flight and overthrown, he ran unto a little rock not far off, and there setting his sword's point to his breast fell upon it, and slew himself, but yet, as it is reported, with the help of his friend that dispatched him.

THE LIFE OF MARCUS BRUTUS

* MARCUS BRUTUS came of that Junius Brutus, for whom the
*ancient Romans made his statue of brass to be set
*up in the Capitol with the images of the kings,
*holding a naked sword in his hand, because he
*had valiantly put down the Tarquins from their kingdom
*of Rome.[1] But that Junius Brutus, being of a sour stern
nature, not softened by reason, being like unto sword
blades of too hard a temper, was so subject to his choler
and malice he bare unto the tyrants, that for their sakes he
caused his own sons to be executed. But this
Marcus Brutus in contrary manner, whose life we
presently write, having framed his manners of life by the
rules of virtue and study of Philosophy, and having employed
his wit, which was gentle and constant, in attempting
of great things: methinks he was rightly made and framed
unto virtue. So that his very enemies which wish him
most hurt, because of his conspiracy against Julius Caesar,
if there were any noble attempt done in all this conspiracy,
they refer it wholly unto Brutus, and all the cruel and
violent acts unto Cassius, who was Brutus' familiar friend,

The parentage of Brutus.

Brutus' manners.

[1] Cf. *Julius Caesar*, I. ii 158-162.

but not so well given and conditioned as he. His mother
Servilia, it is thought, came of the blood of Servilius Ahala, who, when Spurius Maelius went about
to make himself king, and to bring it to pass
had enticed the common people to rebel, took a dagger and
hid it close under his arm, and went into the market place.
When he was come thither, he made as though he had
somewhat to say unto him, and pressed as near him as he
could: wherefore, Maelius stooping down with his head to
hear what he would say, Servilius stabbed him in with his
dagger and slew him. Thus much all writers agree for his
mother. Now touching his father, some for the evil will
and malice they bare unto Brutus, because of the death of
Julius Caesar, do maintain that he came not of Junius
Brutus that drave out the Tarquins: for there were none
left of his race, considering that his two sons were executed
for conspiracy with the Tarquins: and that Marcus Brutus
came of a mean house, the which was raised to honour and
office in the commonwealth but of late time. Posidonius
the Philosopher writeth the contrary, that Junius Brutus
indeed slew two of his sons which were men grown, as the
histories do declare, howbeit that there was a third son,
being but a little child at that time, from whom the house
and family afterwards was derived: and futhermore, that
there were in his time certain famous men of that family,
whose stature and countenance resembled much the image
of Junius Brutus. And thus much for this matter. Marcus

Servilia, M. Brutus' mother.

Cato the Philosopher was brother unto Servilia, M. Brutus' mother: whom Brutus studied most to follow of all the other Romans, because he was his uncle, and afterwards he married his daughter. Now touching the Grecian Philosophers, there was no sect nor Philosopher of them, but he heard and liked it: but above all the rest he loved Plato's sect best, and did not much give himself to the new nor mean Academy as they call it, but altogether to the old Academy. Therefore he did ever greatly esteem the Philosopher Antiochus, of the city of Ascalon: but he was more familiar with his brother Ariston, who for learning and knowledge was inferior to many other Philosophers, but for wisdom and courtesy equal with the best and chiefest. Touching Empylus, whom Marcus Brutus himself doth mention in his Epistles, and his friends also in many places, he was an Orator, and left an excellent book he wrote of the death of Julius Caesar, and titled it *Brutus*. He was properly learned in the Latin tongue, and was able to make long discourse in it, beside that he could also plead very well in Latin. But, for the Greek tongue, they do note in some of his Epistles, that he counterfeited that brief compendious manner of speech of the Lacedaemonians. As, when the war was begun, he wrote unto the Pergamenians in this sort: 'I understand you have given Dolabella money:

Servilia Cato's sister.

Brutus' studies.

Brutus followed the old Academics.

Empylus, an Orator, wrote a book of Caesar's death, and entitled it Brutus

Brutus' manner of writing his Epistles in Greek.

if you have done it willingly, you confess you have offended me: if against your wills, shew it then by giving me willingly.' Another time again unto the Samians: 'Your counsels be long, your doings be slow, consider the end.' And in another Epistle he wrote unto the Patareians: 'The Xanthians, despising my good will, have made their country a grave of despair: and the Patareians, that put themselves into my protection, have lost no jot of their liberty. And therefore, whilst you have liberty, either choose the judgement of the Patareians or the fortune of the Xanthians.' These were Brutus' manner of letters, which were honoured for their briefness. So Brutus being but a young stripling went into Cyprus with his uncle Cato, who was sent against Ptolemy king of Egypt, who having slain himself, Cato, staying for certain necessary business he had in the Isle of Rhodes, had already sent Canidius, one of his friends, before to keep his treasure and goods. But Cato, fearing he would be lightfingered, wrote unto Brutus forthwith to come out of Pamphylia (where he was but newly recovered of a sickness) into Cyprus, the which he did. The which journey he was sorry to take upon him, both for respect of Canidius' shame, whom Cato as he thought wrongfully slandered, as also because he thought this office too mean and unmeet for him, being a young man, and given to his book. This notwithstanding he behaved himself so honestly and carefully that Cato did greatly commend him:

A brief letter to the Samians

Brutus followed Cato into Cyprus.

MARCUS BRUTUS

and after all the goods were sold and converted into ready money, he took the most part of it, and returned withal to Rome. Afterwards when the Empire of Rome was divided into factions, and that Caesar and Pompey both were in arms one against the other, and that all the Empire of Rome was in garboil and uproar: it was thought then that Brutus would take part with Caesar, because Pompey not long before had put his father unto death. But Brutus preferring the respect of his country and commonwealth before private affection, and persuading himself that Pompey had juster cause to enter into arms than Caesar: he then took part with Pompey, though oftentimes meeting him before he thought scorn to speak to him, thinking it a great sin and offence in him to speak to the murtherer of his father. *Brutus taketh part with Pompey.* But then submitting himself unto Pompey, as unto the head of the commonwealth, he sailed into Sicilia, Lieutenant under Sestius that was Governor of that province. But when he saw that there was no way to rise, nor to do any noble exploits, and that Caesar and Pompey were both camped together, and fought for victory: he went of himself unsent for into Macedon to be partaker of the danger. It is reported that Pompey being glad, and wondering at his coming, when he saw him come to him, he rose out of his chair, and went and embraced him before them all, and used him as honourably as he could have done the noblest man that took his part. Brutus, being in Pompey's

camp, did nothing but study all day long, except he were
with Pompey, and not only the days before, but
the self same day also before the great battle was
fought in the fields of Pharsalia, where Pompey
was overthrown. It was in the midst of summer, and the
sun was very hot, besides that the camp was lodged near
unto marishes, and they that carried his tent tarried long
before they came, whereupon, being very weary
with travel, scant any meat came into his mouth
at dinner time. Furthermore, when others slept,
or thought what would happen the morrow after, he fell to
his book, and wrote all day long till night, writing a breviary
of Polybius. It is reported that Caesar did not
forget him, and that he gave his Captains charge
before the battle, that they should beware they
killed not Brutus in fight, and if he yielded willingly unto them, that then they should bring him unto
him : but if he resisted and would not be taken, then that
they should let him go and do him no hurt. Some say
he did this for Servilia's sake, Brutus' mother. For, when
he was a young man, he had been acquainted with
Servilia, who was extremely in love with him.
And because Brutus was born in that time when
their love was hottest, he persuaded himself that he
begat him. For proof hereof the report goeth, that when
the weightiest matters were in hand in the Senate, about the
conspiracy of Catiline, which was likely to have undone the

Brutus' exercise in Pompey's camp

Brutus studied in Pompey's camp.

Julius Caesar careful of Brutus' safety

Julius Caesar loved Servilia, Brutus' mother

MARCUS BRUTUS

city of Rome, Caesar and Cato sate near together, and were both of contrary minds to each other : and then, that in the meantime one delivered Caesar a letter. Caesar took it and read it softly to himself : but Cato cried out upon Caesar, and said he did not well to receive advertisements from enemies. Whereupon the whole Senate began to murmur at it. Then Caesar gave Cato the letter as it was sent him, who read it, and found that it was a love letter sent from his sister Servilia : thereupon he cast it again to Caesar, and said unto him, 'Hold, drunken sop.' When he had done so, he went on with his tale, and maintained his opinion as he did before . so commonly was the love of Servilia known which she bare unto Caesar. So, after Pompey's overthrow at the battle of Pharsalia, and that he fled to the sea, when Caesar came to besiege his camp, Brutus went out of the camp gates unseen of any man, and leapt into a marish full of water and reeds. Then when night was come he crept out, and went unto the city of Larissa : from whence he wrote unto Caesar, who was very glad that he had scaped, and sent for him to come unto him. When Brutus was come, he did not only pardon him, but also kept him always about him, and did as much honour and esteem him as any man he had in his company. Now no man could tell whither Pompey was fled, and all were marvellous desirous to know it : wherefore Caesar walking a good way alone with Brutus, he did ask him which way he thought

Brutus saved by Julius Caesar after the battle of Pharsalia

Pompey took. Caesar perceiving by his talk that Brutus guessed certainly whither Pompey should be fled, he left all other ways, and took his journey directly towards Egypt. Pompey, as Brutus conjectured, was indeed fled into Egypt, but there he was villainously slain. Furthermore, Brutus obtained pardon of Caesar for Cassius: and, defending also the king*a* of Libya's cause, he was overlaid with a world of accusations against him, howbeit, entreating for him, he saved him the best part of his realm and kingdom. They say also that Caesar said, when he heard Brutus plead: 'I know not,' said he, 'what this young man would, but, what he would, he willeth it vehemently.' For, as Brutus' gravity and constant mind would not grant all men their requests that sued unto him, but being moved with reason and discretion did always incline to that which was good and honest, even so, when it was moved to follow any matter, he used a kind of forcible and vehement persuasion, that calmed not till he had obtained his desire. For, by flattering of him, a man could never obtain anything at his hands, nor make him to do that which was unjust. Further, he thought it not meet for a man of calling and estimation to yield unto the requests and entreaties of a shameless and importunate suitor, requesting things unmeet: the which notwithstanding, some men do for shame, because they dare deny nothing. And therefore he was

a This king was Juba. howbeit it is true also that Brutus made intercession for Deïotarus, king of Galatia, who was deprived notwithstanding of the most part of his country by Caesar, and therefore this place were best to be understanded by Deïotarus.

MARCUS BRUTUS

wont to say, that he thought them evil brought up in their youth, that could deny nothing. Now when Caesar took sea to go into Africk against Cato and Scipio, he left Brutus Governor of Gaul in Italy, on this side of the Alps, which was a great good hap for that province. For where others were spoiled and polled by the insolency and covetousness of the Governors, as if it had been a country conquered, Brutus was a comfort and rest unto their former troubles and miseries they sustained. But he referred it wholly unto Caesar's grace and goodness. For when Caesar returned out of Africk, and progressed up and down Italy, the things that pleased him best to see were the cities under Brutus' charge and government, and Brutus himself: who honoured Caesar in person, and whose company also Caesar greatly esteemed. Now there were divers sorts of Praetorships at Rome, and it was looked for, that Brutus or Cassius would make suit for the chiefest Praetorship, which they called the Praetorship of the city: because he that had that office was as a Judge to minister justice unto the citizens. Therefore they strove one against the other, though some say that there was some little grudge betwixt them for other matters before, and that this contention did set them further out, though they were allied together. For Cassius had married Junia, Brutus' sister. Others say, that this contention betwixt them came by Caesar himself, who secretly

[margin: Caesar made Brutus Governor of Gaul on this side the mountains.]

[margin: Brutus and Cassius contend for the Praetorship of the city.]

[margin: Cassius married Junia, Brutus sister]

gave either of them both hope of his favour. So their suit for the Praetorship was so followed and laboured of either party, that one of them put another in suit of law. Brutus with his virtue and good name contended against many noble exploits in arms, which Cassius had done against the Parthians. So Caesar, after he had heard both their objections, he told his friends with whom he consulted about this matter: 'Cassius' cause is the juster,' said he, 'but Brutus must be first preferred.' Thus Brutus had the first Praetorship, and Cassius the second: who thanked not Caesar so much for the Praetorship he had, as he was angry with him for that he had lost. But Brutus in many other things tasted of the benefit of Caesar's favour in anything he requested. For, if he had listed, he might have been one of Caesar's chiefest friends, and of greatest authority and credit about him. Howbeit Cassius' friends did dissuade him from it, (for Cassius and he were not yet reconciled together sithence their first contention and strife for the Praetorship,) and prayed him to beware of Caesar's sweet enticements, and to fly his tyrannical favours: the which they said Caesar gave him, not to honour his virtue but to weaken his constant mind, framing it to the bent of his bow. Now Caesar on the other side did not trust him overmuch, nor was not without tales brought unto him against him: howbeit he feared his great mind, authority, and friends. Yet, on the other side also, he trusted his good nature and

The first cause of Cassius' malice against Caesar

Caesar suspected Brutus.

MARCUS BRUTUS

fair conditions. For, intelligence being brought him one day, that Antonius and Dolabella did conspire against him, he *answered, that these fat long-haired men made him *not afraid, but the lean and whitely-faced fellows, *meaning that by Brutus and Cassius.[1] At another time also when one accused Brutus unto him, and bade him beware of him : 'What,' said he again, clapping his hand on his breast, 'think ye that Brutus will not tarry till this body die?' Meaning that none but Brutus after him was meet to have such power as he had. And surely, in my opinion, I am persuaded that Brutus might indeed have come to have been the chiefest man of Rome, if he could have contented himself for a time to have been next unto Caesar, and to have suffered his glory and authority which he had gotten by his great victories to consume with time. But Cassius being a choleric man, and hating Caesar privately, more than he did the tyranny openly, he incensed Brutus against him. It is also reported that Brutus could evil away with the tyranny, and that Cassius hated the tyrant, making many complaints for the injuries he had done him, and, amongst others, for that he had taken away his Lions from him. Cassius had provided them for his sports, when he should be Aedilis, and they were found in the city of Megara when it was won by Calenus, and Caesar kept them. The rumour went that these Lions did marvellous great hurt to the Megarians For

Caesar's saying of Brutus.

Cassius incenseth Brutus against Caesar.

Cassius' Lions at Megara.

[1] Cf. *Julius Caesar*, I. ii. 191-200.

when the city was taken, they brake their cages where they were tied up, and turned them loose, thinking they would have done great mischief to the enemies, and have kept them from setting upon them: but the Lions, contrary to expectation, turned upon themselves that fled unarmed, and did so cruelly tear some in pieces, that it pitied their enemies to see them. And this was the cause, as some do report, that made Cassius conspire against Caesar. But this holdeth no water. For Cassius even from his cradle could not abide any manner of tyrants, as it appeared when he was but a boy, and went unto the same school that Faustus the son of Sylla did. And Faustus, bragging among other boys, highly boasted of his father's kingdom: Cassius rose up on his feet, and gave him two good whirts on the ear. Faustus' governors would have put this matter in suit against Cassius: but Pompey would not suffer them, but caused the two boys to be brought before him, and asked them how the matter came to pass. Then Cassius, as it is written of him, said unto the other: 'Go to, Faustus, speak again, an thou darest before this nobleman here, the same words that made me angry with thee, that my fists may walk once again about thine ears.' Such was Cassius' hot stirring nature. But for Brutus, his friends* and countrymen, both by divers procurements,* and sundry rumours of the city, and by many bills* also, did openly call and procure him to do that he* did. For, under the image of his ancestor Junius Brutus,*

Cassius an enemy of tyrants.

How Brutus was incensed against Caesar.

MARCUS BRUTUS

*that drave the kings out of Rome, they wrote: 'Oh that it
*pleased the gods thou wert now alive, Brutus': and again,
*'That thou wert here among us now.' His tribunal (or
*chair), where he gave audience during the time he was
*Praetor, was full of such bills: 'Brutus, thou art asleep,
*and art not Brutus indeed.'[1] And of all this Caesar's flatterers were the cause: who beside many other exceeding and unspeakable honours they daily devised for him, in the night time they did put Diadems upon the heads of his images, supposing thereby to allure the common people to call him king, instead of Dictator. Howbeit it turned to the contrary, as we have written more at large in Julius Caesar's life. Now when Cassius felt his friends, and did stir them up against Caesar, they all agreed and promised to take part with him, so Brutus were the chief of their con-
*spiracy. For they told him, that so high an enterprise and
*attempt as that did not so much require men of manhood
*and courage to draw their swords, as it stood them upon to
*have a man of such estimation as Brutus, to make every man
*boldly think that by his only presence the fact were holy and
*just. If he took not this course, then that they should go
*to it with fainter hearts, and when they had done it they
*should be more fearful: because every man would think
*that Brutus would not have refused to have made one with
*them, if the cause had been good and honest.[2] Therefore

[1] Cf. *Julius Caesar*, I. iii. 142–6; *Life of Caesar*, pp. 94, 95.
Cf *Julius Caesar*, I. iii. 157–60.

Cassius, considering this matter with himself, did first of
all speak to Brutus since they grew strange together
for the suit they had for the Praetorship.[1] So
when he was reconciled to him again, and that
they had embraced one another, Cassius asked him
if he were determined to be in the Senate-house,
the first day of the month of March, because he heard say
that Caesar's friends should move the council that day, that
Caesar should be called king by the Senate. Brutus
answered him, he would not be there. 'But if we be sent
for,' said Cassius, 'how then?' 'For myself then,' said
Brutus, 'I mean not to hold my peace, but to withstand it,
and rather die than lose my liberty.' Cassius being bold,
and taking hold of this word, 'Why,' quoth he, 'what
Roman is he alive that will suffer thee to die for the liberty?
What, knowest thou not that thou art Brutus? Thinkest
thou that they be cobblers, tapsters, or suchlike base mechan-
ical people, that write these bills and scrolls which are found
daily in thy Praetor's chair, and not the noblest men and
best citizens that do it? No, be thou well assured, that of
other Praetors they look for gifts, common distributions
amongst the people, and for common plays, and to see fencers fight at the sharp, to shew the people pastime: but at
thy hands they specially require (as a due debt unto them)
the taking away of the tyranny, being fully bent to suffer
any extremity for thy sake, so that thou wilt shew thyself

Cassius prayeth Brutus first to help him to put down the tyrant.

[1] Cf. *Julius Caesar*, I. ii. 32–36.

MARCUS BRUTUS

to be the man thou art taken for, and that they hope thou art.' Thereupon he kissed Brutus and embraced him: and so, each taking leave of other, they went both to speak *with their friends about it. Now amongst Pompey's friends *there was one called Caius*a* Ligarius, who had *been accused unto Caesar for taking part with *Pompey, and Caesar discharged him. But <u>Ligarius</u> *thanked not Caesar so much <u>for his discharge,</u> as he was *<u>offended</u> with him for that he was brought in danger by his *<u>tyrannical power</u>.[1] And therefore in his heart he was alway his mortal enemy, and was besides very familiar with Brutus, who went to see him being sick in his bed, and said unto †him: 'O Ligarius, in what a time art thou †sick?' Ligarius rising up in his bed, and taking †him by the right hand, said unto him: 'Brutus,' †said he, 'if thou hast any great enterprise in hand †worthy of thyself, I am whole.'[2] After that time they began to feel all their acquaintance whom they trusted, and laid their heads together consulting upon it, and did not only pick out their friends, but all those also whom they thought stout enough to attempt any desperate matter, and that were not afraid to lose *their lives. For this cause they durst not acquaint *Cicero with their conspiracy, although he was a *man whom they loved dearly, and trusted best: for they

a In another place they call him Quintus.

Brutus maketh Ligarius one of the conspiracy.

They do hide the conspiracy against Caesar from Cicero.

[1] Cf. *Julius Caesar*, II. i. 215-16.
[2] *Ibid.* II. i. 314-17.

were afraid that he being a coward by nature, and age*
also having increased his fear, he would quite turn and*
alter all their purpose, and quench the heat of their enter-*
prise, the which specially required hot and earnest execution,*
seeking by persuasion to bring all things to such safety,*
as there should be no peril.[1] Brutus also did let other of*
his friends alone as Statilius Epicurean, and Favonius that
made profession to follow Marcus Cato. Because that
having cast out words afar off, disputing together in
Philosophy to feel their minds, Favonius answered that
civil war was worse than tyrannical government
usurped against the law. And Statilius told him
also that it were an unwise part of him, to put his
life in danger for a sight of ignorant fools and
asses. Labeo was present at this talk, and maintained the
contrary against them both. But Brutus held his peace,
as though it had been a doubtful matter, and a hard thing
to have decided. But afterwards, being out of their company, he made Labeo privy to his intent: who very readily
offered himself to make one. And they thought good also
to bring in another Brutus to join with him, surnamed
Albinus: who was no man of his hands himself, but because
he was able to bring good force of a great number of slaves,
and fencers at the sharp, whom he kept to shew the people
pastime with their fighting, besides also that Caesar had
some trust in him. Cassius and Labeo told Brutus Albinus

Civil war worse than tyrannical government.

[1] Cf. *Julius Caesar*, II. i. 141–52.

of it at the first, but he made them no answer. But when he had spoken with Brutus himself alone, and that Brutus had told him he was the chief ringleader of all this conspiracy, then he willingly promised him the best aid he could. Furthermore, the only name and great calling of Brutus did bring on the most of them to give consent to this conspiracy. Who having never taken oaths together, nor taken or given any caution or assurance, nor binding themselves one to another by any religious oaths :[1] they all kept the matter so secret to themselves, and could so cunningly handle it, that notwithstanding the gods did reveal it by manifest signs and tokens from above, and by predictions of sacrifices, yet all this would not be believed. Now Brutus, who knew very well that for his sake all the noblest, valiantest, and most courageous men of Rome did venture their lives, weighing with himself the greatness of the danger: when he was out of his house, he did so frame and fashion his countenance and looks, that no man could discern he had anything to trouble his mind. But when night came that he was in his own house, then he was clean changed. For either care did wake him against his will when he would have slept, or else oftentimes of himself he fell into such deep thoughts of this enterprise, casting in his mind all the dangers that might happen, that his wife, lying by him, found that there was some marvellous great matter that

The wonderful faith and secrecy of the Conspirators of Caesar's death.

[1] Cf. *Julius Caesar*, II. i. 114-40.

troubled his mind, not being wont to be in that taking, and*
that he could not well determine with himself.[1] *

Porcia Cato's daughter wife unto Brutus.

His wife Porcia (as we have told you before) was
the daughter of Cato, whom Brutus married being
his cousin, not a maiden, but a young widow after
the death of her first husband Bibulus, by whom she had

Bibulus' book of Brutus' acts.

also a young son called Bibulus, who afterwards
wrote a book of the acts and gests of Brutus, extant
at this present day. This young Lady being
excellently well seen in Philosophy, loving her husband well,

Porcia studied in Philosophy.

and being of a noble courage, as she was also wise;
because she would not ask her husband what he
ailed before she had made some proof by her self,
she took a little razor such as barbers occupy to pare men's

The courage of Porcia

nails, and, causing all her maids and women to go
out of her chamber, gave her self a great gash
withal in her thigh, that she was straight all of a gore-
blood, and incontinently after a vehement fever took her, by

Great difference betwixt a wife and a harlot. Porcia's words unto her husband Brutus

reason of the pain of her wound. Then perceiving
her husband was marvellously out of quiet, and that
he could take no rest, even in her greatest pain of
all she spake in this sort unto him: 'I being, O*
'Brutus,' (said she) 'the daughter of Cato, was*
'married unto thee, not to be thy bedfellow and*
'companion in bed and at board only, like a harlot,*
but to be partaken also with thee of thy good and evil*

[1] Cf. *Julius Caesar*, II. i. 237-55.

"'fortune. Now for thyself, I can find no cause of fault
"'in thee touching our match : but for my part, how may
"'I shew my duty towards thee, and how much I would do
"'for thy sake, if I cannot constantly bear a secret mischance
"'or grief with thee, which requireth secrecy and fidelity ?
"'I confess that a woman's wit commonly is too weak to
"'keep a secret safely : but yet, Brutus, good education and
"'the company of virtuous men have some power to reform
"'the defect of nature. And for myself, I have this benefit
"'moreover : that I am the daughter of Cato, and wife of
"'Brutus. This notwithstanding, I did not trust to any of
"'these things before : until that now I have found by
"'experience, that no pain nor grief whatsoever can over-
"'come me.' With those words she shewed him her
"wound on her thigh, and told him what she had done to
"prove her self. Brutus was amazed to hear what she said
"unto him, and lifting up his hands to heaven, he besought
"the gods to give him the grace he might bring his enterprise
"to so good pass, that he might be found a husband worthy
"of so noble a wife as Porcia : so he then did comfort her the
"best he could.[1] Now a day being appointed for the meeting
of the Senate, at what time they hoped Caesar would not
fail to come, the conspirators determined then to put their
enterprise in execution, because they might meet safely at
that time without suspicion, and the rather, for that all the
noblest and chiefest men of the city would be there. Who,

[1] Cf. *Julius Caesar*, II. i. 280-7, 292-303, 305-8.

when they should see such a great matter executed, would every man then set-to their hands for the defence of their liberty. Furthermore, they thought also that the appointment of the place where the council should be kept, was chosen of purpose by divine providence, and made all for them. For it was one of the porches about the Theatre, in the which there was a certain place full of seats for men to sit in, where also was set up the image of Pompey, which the city had made and consecrated in honour of him, when he did beautify that part of the city with the Theatre he built, with diverse porches about it. In this place was the assembly of the Senate appointed to be, just on the fifteenth day of the month of March, which the Romans call *Idus Martias*: so that it seemed some god of purpose had brought Caesar thither to be slain, for revenge of Pompey's death. So, when the day was come, Brutus went out of his house with a dagger by his side under his long gown, that nobody saw nor knew, but his wife only. The other conspirators were all assembled at Cassius' house, to bring his son into the market place, who on that day did put on the man's gown, called *Toga Virilis*, and from thence they came all in a troop together unto Pompey's porch, looking that Caesar would straight come thither. But here is to be noted the wonderful assured constancy of these conspirators, in so dangerous and weighty an enterprise as they had undertaken. For many of them being Praetors, by reason of their office,

The wonderful constancy of the conspirators in killing of Caesar.

whose duty is to minister justice to everybody, they did not only with great quietness and courtesy hear them that spake unto them, or that pleaded matters before them, and gave them attentive ear, as if they had had no other matter in their heads: but moreover, they gave just sentence, and carefully despatched the causes before them. So there was one among them, who being condemned in a certain sum of money refused to pay it, and cried out that he did appeal unto Caesar. Then Brutus, casting his eyes upon the conspirators, said, 'Caesar shall not let me to see the law executed.' Notwithstanding this, by chance there fell out many misfortunes unto them, which was enough to have marred the enterprise. The first and chiefest was Caesar's long tarrying, who came very late to the Senate: for, because the signs of the sacrifices appeared unlucky, his wife Calpurnia kept him at home, and the Soothsayers bade him beware he went not abroad. The second cause was when one came unto Casca being a conspirator, and, taking him by the hand, said unto him: 'O Casca, thou keptest it close from me, but Brutus hath told me all.' Casca being amazed at it, the other went on with his tale, and said: 'Why, how now, how cometh it to pass thou art thus rich, that thou dost sue to be Aedilis?' Thus Casca being deceived by the other's doubtful words, he told them it was a thousand to one, he blabbed not out all the conspiracy. Another Senator called Popillius Laena, after he had saluted Brutus

Sundry misfortunes to have broken off the enterprise.

and Cassius more friendly than he was wont to do, he rounded softly in their ears, and told them, 'I pray the gods you may go through with that you have taken in hand, but withal dispatch, I read you, for your enterprise is bewrayed.' When he had said, he presently departed from them, and left them both afraid that their conspiracy would out.[1] Now in the meantime, there came one of Brutus' men post-haste unto him, and told him his wife was a-dying.

<small>The weakness of Porcia not withstanding her former courage</small>

For Porcia being very careful and pensive for that which was to come, and being too weak to away with so great and inward grief of mind: she could hardly keep within, but was frighted with every little noise and cry she heard, as those that are taken and possessed with the fury of the Bacchantes, asking every man that came from the market place, what Brutus did, and still sent messenger after messenger, to know what news.[2] At length, Caesar's coming being prolonged as you have heard, Porcia's weakness was not able to hold out any lenger, and thereupon she suddenly swooned, that she had no leisure to go to her chamber, but was taken in the midst of her house, where her speech and senses failed her. Howbeit she soon came to her self again, and so was laid in her bed, and tended by her women. When Brutus heard these news, it grieved him, as it is to be presupposed: yet he left not off the care of his country and commonwealth, neither went home to his house for any news he heard.

[1] Cf. *Julius Caesar*, III. i.   [2] *Ibid.* I iv. 13-17.

Now, it was reported that Caesar was coming in his litter, for he determined not to stay in the Senate all that day (because he was afraid of the unlucky signs of the sacrifices) but to adjourn matters of importance unto the next session and council holden, feigning himself not to be well at ease.
*When Caesar came out of his litter, Popillius Laena, that had
*talked before with Brutus and Cassius, and had prayed the
*gods they might bring this enterprise to pass, went unto
*Caesar, and kept him a long time with a talk. Caesar gave
*good ear unto him. Wherefore the conspirators (if so they
*should be called) not hearing what he said to Caesar, but
*conjecturing by that he had told them a little before, that
*his talk was none other but the very discovery of their
*conspiracy. they were afraid every man of them, and one
*looking in another's face, it was easy to see that they all
*were of a mind that it was no tarrying for them till they
*were apprehended, but rather that they should kill them-
*selves with their own hands. And when Cassius and
*certain other clapped their hands on their swords under
*their gowns to draw them, Brutus marking the countenance
*and gesture of Laena, and considering that he did use him-
*self rather like an humble and earnest suitor than
*like an accuser, he said nothing to his companion
*(because there were many amongst them that were
*not of the conspiracy) but with a pleasant counten-
*ance encouraged Cassius. And immediately after
*Laena went from Caesar, and kissed his hand: which

Brutus with his countenance encouraged his fearful consorts.

shewed plainly that it was for some matter concerning himself, that he had held him so long in talk.¹ Now all the Senators being entered first into this place or chapter-house where the council should be kept, all the other conspirator straight stood about Caesar's chair, as if they had had something to have said unto him. And some say that Cassius casting his eyes upon Pompey's image, made his prayer unto it, as if it had been alive. Trebonius,ᵃ on th' other side, drew Antonius at o' side as he came into the house where the Senate sat, and held him with a long talk without.² When Caesar was come into the house, all the house rose to honour him at his coming in. So, when he was set, the conspirator flocked about him, and amongst them they presented one Tullius, Cimber, who made humble suit for the calling home again of his brother that was banished. They all made as though they were intercessors for him, and took him by the hand and kissed his head and breast. Caesar at the first simply refused their kindness and entreaties: but afterwards perceiving they still pressed on him, he violently thrust them from him. Then Cimber with both his hands plucked Caesar's gown over his shoulders and Casca that stood behind him drew his dagger first, and

ᵃIn Caesar's life it is said it was Decius Brutus Albinus that kept Antonius with a talk without.

ᵇIn Caesar's life he is called Metellus Cimber.

The murther of Caesar.

¹ Cf. *Julius Caesar*, III. 1. 18-24.
² *Julius Caesar*, III. i. 25, 6; *Life of Caesar*, p. 100; *Life of Antony* Vol. II. pp 20, 21.

MARCUS BRUTUS

strake Caesar upon the shoulder, but gave him no great wound. Caesar, feeling himself hurt, took him straight by the hand he held his dagger in, and cried out in Latin : ' O traitor Casca, what doest thou ?' Casca on th' other side cried in Greek, and called his brother to help him. So divers running on a heap together to fly upon Caesar, he looking about him to have fled, saw Brutus with a sword drawn in his hand ready to strike at him · then he let Casca's hand go, and, casting his gown over his face, suffered every man to strike at him that would. Then the conspirators thronging one upon another because every man was desirous to have a cut at him, so many swords and daggers lighting upon one body, one of them hurt another, and among them Brutus caught a blow on his hand, because he would make one in murdering of him, and all the rest also were every man of them bloodied. Caesar being slain in this manner, Brutus, standing in the midst of the house, would have spoken and stayed the other Senators that were not of the conspiracy, to have told them the reason why they had done this fact. But they, as men both afraid and amazed, fled one upon another's neck in haste to get out at the door, and no man followed them. For it was set down and agreed between them that they should kill no man but Caesar only, and should entreat all the rest to look to defend their *liberty. All the conspirators but Brutus, determining upon *this matter, thought it good also to kill Antonius, because *he was a wicked man, and that in nature favoured tyranny :

Casca the first that wounded him.

besides also, for that he was in great estimation with soldiers, having been conversant of long time amongst them: and specially having a mind bent to great enterprises, he was also of great authority at that time, being Consul with Caesar. But Brutus would not agree to it.[1] First, for that he said it was not honest: secondly, because he told them there was hope of change in him. For he did not mistrust, but that Antonius, being a noble-minded and courageous man, (when he should know that Caesar was dead) would willingly help his country to recover her liberty, having them an example unto him, to follow their courage and virtue. So Brutus by this means saved Antonius' life, who at that present time disguised himself and stale away. But Brutus and his consorts, having their swords bloody in their hands, went straight to the Capitol, persuading the Romans as they went to take their liberty again. Now, at the first time when the murther was newly done, there were sudden outcries of people that ran up and down the city, the which indeed did the more increase the fear and tumult. But when they saw they slew no man, neither did spoil or make havoc of anything, then certain of the Senators and many of the people, emboldening themselves, went to the Capitol unto them. There a great number of men being assembled together one after another,

Why Antonius was not slain with Caesar

Brutus with his consorts went unto the Capitol

[1] Cf. *Julius Caesar*, II. i. 155–66, 181–5; *Life of Antonius*, Vol. II. p. 20.

MARCUS BRUTUS

Brutus made an oration unto them to win the favour of the people, and to justify that they had done. All those that were by said they had done well, and cried unto them that they should boldly come down from the Capitol. Whereupon, Brutus and his companions came boldly down into the *market place. The rest followed in troop, but Brutus went *foremost, very honourably compassed in round about with *the noblest men of the city, which brought him from the *Capitol, through the market place, to the pulpit for ora-*tions. When the people saw him in the pulpit, although *they were a multitude of rakehells of all sorts, and had a *good will to make some stir: yet being ashamed to do it for *the reverence they bare unto Brutus, they kept silence, to *hear what he would say. When Brutus began to speak, *they gave him quiet audience [1]: howbeit immediately after, they shewed that they were not all contented with the murther. For when another called Cinna would have spoken, and began to accuse Caesar, they fell into a great uproar among them, and marvellously reviled him. Insomuch that the conspirators returned again into the Capitol. There Brutus, being afraid to be besieged, sent back again *the noblemen that came thither with him, thinking it no *reason that they, which were no partakers of the murther, *should be partakers of the danger.[2] Then the next morning the Senate being assembled, and holden within the temple of the goddess Tellus, to wit, the earth, and Antonius,

[1] Cf. *Julius Caesar*, III. ii. 1–11.   [2] *Ibid.* III. i. 94, 5.

Plancus, and Cicero having made a motion to the Senate in that assembly, that they should take an order to pardon and forget all that was past, and to stablish friendship and peace again : it was decreed, that they should not only be pardoned, but also that the Consuls should refer it to the Senate what honours should be appointed unto them. This being agreed upon, the Senate brake up, and Antonius the Consul, to put them in heart that were in the Capitol, sent them his son for a pledge. Upon this assurance, Brutus and his companions came down from the Capitol, where every man saluted and embraced each other, among the which Antonius himself did bid Cassius to supper to him : and Lepidus also bade Brutus, and so one bade another, as they had friendship and acquaintance together. The next day following, the Senate being called again to council did first of all commend Antonius, for that he had wisely stayed and quenched the beginning of a civil war : then they also gave Brutus and his consorts great praises, and lastly they appointed them several governments of provinces. For unto Brutus, they appointed Creta : Africk, unto Cassius : Asia, unto Trebonius : Bithynia, unto Cimber : and unto the other Decius Brutus Albinus, Gaul on this side the Alps. When this was done, they came to talk of Caesar's will and testament, and of his funerals and tomb. Then Antonius thinking good his testament should be read openly, and also that his body should be honourably

Honours decreed for the murtherers of Caesar.

Caesar's will & funerals.

buried, and not in hugger mugger, lest the people might thereby take occasion to be worse offended if they did otherwise: Cassius stoutly spake against it. But Brutus went with the motion, and agreed unto it: wherein it seemeth he committed a second fault. For the first fault he did was when he would not consent to his fellow-conspirators, that Antonius should be slain: and therefore he was justly accused, that thereby he had saved and strengthened a strong and grievous enemy of their conspiracy. The second fault was when he agreed that Caesar's funerals should be as Antonius would †have them: the which indeed marred all. For first of all, †when Caesar's testament was openly read among them, †whereby it appeared that he bequeathed unto every Citizen †of Rome 75 Drachmas a man, and that he left his gardens †and arbours unto the people, which he had on this side of †the river of Tiber, in the place where now the temple †of Fortune is built: the people then loved him, and were †marvellous sorry for him.[1] Afterwards, when *Caesar's body was brought into the market place, *Antonius making his funeral oration in praise of *the dead, according to the ancient custom of Rome, and *perceiving that his words moved the common people to *compassion: he framed his eloquence to make their hearts *yearn the more, and, taking Caesar's gown all bloody in his

Brutus committed two great faults after Caesar's death.

Antonius' funeral oration for Caesar.

[1] Cf. *Julius Caesar*, III. ii. 245-56; *Life of Caesar*, p. 104; *Life of Antonius*, Vol. II. p. 23, 24.

hand, he laid it open to the sight of them all, shewing
what a number of cuts and holes it had upon it. Therewithal the people fell presently into such a rage and mutiny, that there was no more order kept amongst the common people. For some of them cried out, 'Kill the murtherers:'[1] others plucked up forms, tables, and stalls about the market place, as they had done before at the funerals of Clodius, and having laid them all on a heap together they set them on fire, and thereupon did put the body of Caesar, and burnt it in the midst of the most holy places. And furthermore, when the fire was thoroughly kindled, some here, some there, took burning firebrands, and ran with them to the murtherers' houses that had killed him, to set them afire.[2] Howbeit the conspirators, foreseeing the danger before, had wisely provided for themselves, and fled.[3]

The strange dream of Cinna the Poet.

But there was a Poet called Cinna, who had been no partaker of the conspiracy, but was alway one of Caesar's chiefest friends: he dreamed the night before that Caesar bade him to supper with him, and that he refusing to go, Caesar was very importunate with him, and compelled him, so that at length he led him by the hand into a great dark place, where being marvellously afraid, he was driven to follow him in

---

[1] Cf. *Julius Caesar*, III. ii. 45-210; *Life of Antonius*, Vol. II. p. 22.
[2] Cf. *Julius Caesar*, III. ii. 258-64; *Life of Caesar*, p. 104; *Life of Antonius*, Vol. II. p. 22.
[3] Cf. *Julius Caesar*, III. ii. 273, 4; *Life of Antonius*, Vol. II. p. 22

*spite of his heart. This dream put him all night into a
*fever, and yet notwithstanding, the next morning when he
*heard that they carried Caesar's body to burial, being
*ashamed not to accompany his funerals: he went out of his
*house, and thrust himself into the press of the common
*people that were in a great uproar. And because
*some one called him by his name, Cinna, the
*people thinking he had been that Cinna, who
*in an oration he made had spoken very evil of
*Caesar, they falling upon him in their rage slew
*him outright in the market place.[1] This made
Brutus and his companions more afraid than any
other thing, next unto the change of Antonius.
Wherefore they got them out of Rome, and kept
at the first in the city of Antium, hoping to return again
to Rome, when the fury of the people were a little
assuaged. The which they hoped would be quickly, considering that they had to deal with a fickle and unconstant
multitude, easy to be carried, and that the Senate stood
for them: who notwithstanding made no inquiry of
them that had torn poor Cinna the Poet in pieces, but
caused them to be sought for and apprehended that went
with firebrands to set fire of the conspirators' houses.
The people growing weary now of Antonius' pride and
insolency, who ruled all things in manner with absolute
power: they desired that Brutus might return again, and

The murder of Cinna the Poet, being mistaken for another of that name Brutus and his consorts do fly from Rome

[1] Cf. *Julius Caesar*, III iii.; *Life of Caesar*, p. 105.

it was also looked for, that Brutus would come himself in person to play the plays which were due to the people, by reason of his office of Praetorship. But Brutus understanding that many of Ceasar's soldiers which served under him in the wars, and that also had lands and houses given them in the cities where they lay, did lie in wait for him to kill him, and that they daily by small companies came by one and by one into Rome: he durst no more return thither, but yet the people had the pleasure and pastime in his absence, to see the games and sports he made them, which were sumptuously set forth and furnished with all things necessary, sparing for no cost. For he had bought a great number of strange beasts, of the which he would not give one of them to any friend he had, but that they should all be employed in his games: and went himself as far as Byzantium, to speak to some players of comedies and Musicians that were there. And further, he wrote unto his friends for one Canutius an excellent player, that, whatsoever they did, they should entreat him to play in these plays: 'For,' said he, 'it is no reason to compel any Grecian, unless he will come of his own good will.' Moreover, he wrote also unto Cicero, and earnestly prayed him in any case to be at these plays. Now the state of Rome standing in these terms, there fell out another change and alteration, when the young man Octavius Caesar came to Rome. He was the son of Julius Caesar's niece, whom he had

Brutus' plays and sports at Rome in his absence.

Octavius Caesar's coming to Rome.

adopted for his son, and made his heir by his last will and testament. But when Julius Caesar his adopted father was slain, he was in the city of Apollonia where he studied, tarrying for him, because he was determined to make war with the Parthians : but when he heard the news of his death, he returned again to Rome, where to begin to curry favour with the common people, he first of all took upon him his adopted father's name, and made distribution among them of the money which his father had bequeathed unto them. By this means he troubled Antonius sorely, and by force of money got a great number of his father's soldiers together, that had served in the wars with him. And Cicero himself, for the great malice he bare Antonius, did favour his proceedings. But Brutus marvellously reproved him for it, and wrote unto him, that he seemed by his doings not to be sorry to have a Master, but only to be afraid to have one that should hate him : and that all his doings in the commonwealth did witness that he chose to be subject to a mild and courteous bondage, sith by his words and writings he did commend this young man Octavius Caesar to be a good and gentle Lord. 'For our predecessors,' said he, 'would never abide to be subject to any Masters, how gentle or mild soever they were.' and, for his own part, that he had never resolutely determined with himself to make war, or peace, but otherwise, that he was certainly minded never to be slave nor subject. And

<small>Brutus reproved Cicero for taking part with Octavius Caesar.</small>

therefore he wondered much at him, how Cicero could be afraid of the danger of civil wars, and would not be afraid of a shameful peace: and that to thrust Antonius out of the usurped tyranny, in recompense he went about to stablish young Octavius Caesar tyrant. These were the contents of Brutus' first letters he wrote unto Cicero. Now, the city of Rome being divided in two factions, some taking part with Antonius, other also leaning unto Octavius Caesar, and the soldiers making portsale of their service to him that would give most: Brutus seeing the state of Rome would be utterly overthrown, he determined to go out of Italy, and went afoot through the country of Luke unto the city of Elea, standing by the sea. There Porcia, being ready to depart from her husband Brutus and to return to Rome, did what she could to dissemble the grief and sorrow she felt at her heart: but a certain painted table bewrayed her in the end, although until that time she always shewed a constant and patient mind. The device of the table was taken out of the Greek stories, how Andromaché accompanied her husband Hector, when he went out of the city of Troy to go to the wars, and how Hector delivered her his little son, and how her eyes were never off him. Porcia seeing this picture, and likening herself to be in the same case, she fell a-weeping: and coming thither oftentimes in a day to see it, she wept still. Acilius, one of Brutus' friends, perceiving that,

Porcia's sorrowful return to Rome for the absence of her husband Brutus

The story of Hector and Andromaché set forth in painted tables.

MARCUS BRUTUS

rehearsed the verses Andromaché speaketh to this purpose in Homer :

> Thou, Hector, art my father, and my mother, and my brother,
> And husband eke, and all in all : I mind not any other.

Then Brutus, smiling, answered again · 'But yet' (said he) 'I cannot for my part say unto Porcia, as Hector answered Andromaché in the same place of the poet :

> Tush, meddle thou with weighing duly out
> Thy maids their task, and pricking on a clout.

For indeed the weak constitution of her body doth not suffer her to perform in shew the valiant acts that we are able to do : but, for courage and constant mind, she shewed her self as stout in the defence of her country, as any of us.' Bibulus, the son of Porcia, reporteth this story thus. Now Brutus embarking at Elea in Luke, he sailed directly towards Athens. When he arrived there, the people of Athens received him with common joys of rejoicing, and honourable decrees made for him. He lay with a friend of his, with whom he went daily to hear the lectures of Theomnestus Academic Philosopher, and of Cratippus the Peripatetic, and so would talk with them in Philosophy, that it seemed he left all other matters, and gave himself only unto study : howbeit secretly, notwithstanding, he made preparation for war. For he sent Herostratus into Macedon, to win the Captains and soldiers that were upon those marches, and he did also

How Brutus bestowed his time at Athens.

entertain all the young gentlemen of the Romans, whom he found in Athens studying Philosophy: amongst them he found Cicero's son, whom he highly praised and commended, saying, that whether he waked or slept he found him of a noble mind and disposition, he did in nature so much hate tyrants. Shortly after, he began to enter openly into arms: and being advertised that there came out of Asia a certain fleet of Roman ships that had good store of money in them, and that the Captain of those ships (who was an honest man, and his familiar friend) came towards Athens, he went to meet him as far as the Isle of Carystos, and having spoken with him there, he handled him so, that he was contented to leave his ships in his hands. Whereupon he made him a notable banquet at his house, because it was on his birthday. When the feast day came, and that they began to drink lustily one to another, the guests drank to the victory of Brutus, and the liberty of the Romans. Brutus therefore, to encourage them further, called for a bigger cup, and holding it in his hand, before he drank spake this aloud:

> My destiny and Phœbus are agreed,
> To bring me to my final end with speed.

And for proof hereof it is reported, that the same day he fought his last battle by the city of Philippi, as he came out of his tent he gave his men for the word and signal of battle, *Phœbus*: so that it was thought ever since, that this

MARCUS BRUTUS

his sudden crying out at the feast was a prognostication of his misfortune that should happen. After this, Antistius gave him of the money he carried into Italy 50 Myriads. Furthermore, all Pompey's soldiers that straggled up and down Thessaly came with very good will unto him. He took from Cinna also five hundred horsemen, which he carried into Asia, unto Dolabella. After that, he went by sea unto the city of Demetriad, and there took a great deal of armour and munition which was going to Antonius, and the which had been made and forged there by Julius Caesar's commandment, for the wars against the Parthians. Furthermore, Hortensius, governor of Macedon, did resign the government thereof unto him. Besides, all the Princes, kings, and noblemen thereabouts came and joined with him, when it was told him that Caius (Antonius' brother) coming out of Italy, had passed the sea, and came with great speed towards the city of Dyrrachium and Apollonia, to get the soldiers into his hands which Gabinius had there. Brutus therefore, to prevent him, went presently with a few of his men in the midst of winter when it snew hard, and took his way through hard and foul countries, and made such speed indeed, that he was there long before Antonius' sumpters that carried the victuals. So that, when he came near unto Dyrrachium, a disease took him which the physicians call βουλιμία, to say, a cormorant and unsatiable appetite to eat: by reason of the cold and pains he

A strange disease took Brutus at Dyrrachium.

VOL. I. L

had taken. This sickness chanceth often both to men and beasts that travel when it hath snowen : either because the natural heat being retired into the inward parts of the body, by the coldness of the air hardening the skin, doth straight disgest and consume the meat : or else because a sharp subtle wind coming by reason of the snow when it is molten doth pierce into the body, and driveth out the natural heat which was cast outward. For it seemeth that the heat being quenched with the cold, which it meeteth witha coming out of the skin of the body, causeth the sweats that follow the disease. But hereof we have spoken at large in other places. Brutus being very faint, and having nothing in his camp to eat, his soldiers were compelled to go to their enemies, and, coming to the gates of the city they prayed the warders to help them to bread. When they heard in what case Brutus was, they brought him both meat and drink : in requital whereof afterwards, when he wan the city, he did not only entreat and use the Citizens thereof courteously, but all the inhabitants of the city also for their sakes. Now, when Caius Antonius was arrived in the city of Apollonia, he sent unto the soldiers thereabouts to come unto him. But, when he understood that they went all to Brutus, and furthermore that the Citizens of Apollonia did favour him much, he then forsook that city, and went unto the city of Buthrotum but yet he lost three of his ensigns by the way, that were

marginalia: Why by snow this hungry disease taketh men that are wearied with travel.

marginalia: Brutus' thankfulness and clemency

MARCUS BRUTUS 147

slain every man of them. Then he sought by force to win certain places of strength about Byllis, and to drive Brutus' men from thence, that had taken it before: and therefore, to obtain his purpose, he fought a battle with Cicero, the son of Marcus Tullius Cicero, by whom he was overcome. For Brutus made the younger Cicero a Captain, and did many notable exploits by his service. Shortly after, having stolen upon Caius Antonius in certain marishes far from the place from whence he fled, he would not set on him with fury, but only rode round about him, commanding his soldiers to spare him and his men, as reckoning them all his own without stroke striking: and so indeed it happened. For they yielded themselves, and their Captain Antonius, unto Brutus: so that Brutus had now a great army about him. Now Brutus kept this Caius Antonius long time in his office, and never took from him the marks and signs of his Consulship, although many of his friends, and Cicero among others, wrote unto him to put him to death. But when he saw Antonius secretly practised with his Captains to make some alteration, then he sent him into a ship, and made him to be kept there. When the soldiers whom C. Antonius had corrupted were gotten into the city of Apollonia, and sent from thence unto Brutus to come unto them: he made them answer, that it was not the manner of Roman Captains to come to the soldiers, but the soldiers to come to the Captain, and to crave pardon for their offences committed. Thereupon they

C. Antonius yielded unto Brutus.

came to him, and he pardoned them. So, Brutus preparing to go into Asia, news came unto him of the great change at Rome. For Octavius Caesar was in arms, by commandment and authority from the Senate, against Marcus Antonius. But after that he had driven Antonius out of Italy, the Senate then began to be afraid of him: because he sued to be Consul, which was contrary to the law, and kept a great army about him, when the Empire of Rome had no need of them. On the other side, Octavius Caesar perceiving the Senate stayed not there, but turned unto Brutus that was out of Italy, and that they appointed him the government of certain provinces: then he begun to be afraid for his part, and sent unto Antonius to offer him his friendship. *Octavius Caesar joineth with Antonius.* Then coming on with his army near to Rome, he made himself to be chosen Consul, whether the Senate would or not, when he was yet but a stripling or springal of twenty year old, as himself reporteth in his own commentaries. *Brutus accused and condemned by Octavius Caesar's means for the death of Julius Caesar.* So, when he was Consul, he presently appointed Judges to accuse Brutus and his companions, for killing of the noblest person in Rome, and chiefest Magistrate, without law or judgement: and made L. Cornificius accuse Brutus, and M. Agrippa, Cassius. So the parties accused were condemned, because the Judges were compelled to give such sentence. The voice went, that when the Herald (according to the custom after sentence given) went up to the chair or pulpit for

MARCUS BRUTUS

orations, and proclaimed Brutus with a loud voice, summoning him to appear in person before the Judges, the people that stood by sighed openly, and the noblemen that were present hung down their heads, and durst not speak a word. *Among them, the tears fell from Publius Silicius' eyes: *who, shortly after, was one of the proscripts or outlaws *appointed to be slain.[1] After that, these three, *Octavius Caesar, Antonius, and Lepidus, made an *agreement between themselves, aud by those *articles, divided the provinces belonging to the Empire of *Rome among themselves, and did set up bills of proscription *and outlawry, condemning two hundred of the noblest men *of Rome to suffer death,[2] and among that number Cicero *was one.[3] News being brought thereof into Macedon, Brutus being then enforced to it, wrote unto Hortensius that he should put Caius Antonius to death, to be revenged of the death of Cicero, and of the other Brutus, of the which the one was his friend, and the other his kinsman. For this cause therefore, Antonius afterwards taking Hortensius at the battle of Philippi, he made him to be slain upon his brother's tomb. But then Brutus said, that he was more ashamed of the cause for the which Cicero was slain, than he was otherwise sorry for his death: and that he could not but greatly reprove his friends he had at Rome, who were slaves more through their own

The Triumvirate

C. Antonius murdered

[1] Cf. *Julius Caesar*, IV. i. 4, 5.   [2] *Ibid.* IV. i. 1-9.
[3] *Ibid.* IV. iii. 177-9.

fault, than through their valiantness or manhood which usurped the tyranny: considering that they were so cowardly and faint-hearted, as to suffer the sight of those things before their eyes, the report whereof should only have grieved them to the heart. Now when Brutus had passed over his army (that was very great) into Asia, he gave order for the gathering of a great number of ships together, as well in the coast of Bithynia, as also in the city of Cyzicus, because he would have an army by sea: and himself in the meantime went unto the cities, taking order for all things, and giving audience unto Princes and noblemen of the country that had to do with him. Afterwards he sent unto Cassius in Syria, to turn him from his journey into Egypt, telling him that it was not for the conquest of any kingdom for themselves that they wandered up and down in that sort, but contrarily, that it was to restore their country again to their liberty: and that the multitude of soldiers they gathered together was to subdue the tyrants that would keep them in slavery and subjection. Wherefore, regarding their chief purpose and intent, they should not be far from Italy, as near as they could possible, but should rather make all the haste they could to help their countrymen. Cassius believed him, and returned.

Brutus and Cassius do join armies together.

Brutus went to meet him, and they both met at the city of Smyrna, which was the first time that they saw together since they took leave each of other at the haven of Piraeus in Athens: the one going into Syria,

MARCUS BRUTUS 151

and the other into Macedon. So they were marvellous joyful, and no less courageous, when they saw the great armies together which they had both levied : considering that they departing out of Italy like naked and poor banished men, without armour and money, nor having any ship ready, nor soldier about them, nor any one town at their commandment : yet notwithstanding, in a short time after they were now met together, having ships, money, and soldiers enow, both footmen and horsemen, to fight for the Empire of Rome. Now Cassius would have done Brutus as much honour, as Brutus did unto him : but Brutus most commonly prevented him, and went first unto *him, both because he was the elder man,[1] as also for that he *was sickly of body. And men reputed him com- *monly to be very skilful in wars, but otherwise *marvellous choleric and cruel,[2] who sought to rule men by fear, rather than with lenity : and on the other side he was too familiar with his friends, and would jest too broadly with them. But Brutus in contrary manner, for his virtue and valiantness, was well- beloved of the people and his own, esteemed of noble men, and hated of no man, not so much as of his enemies : because he was a marvellous lowly and gentle *person, noble-minded, and would never be in any rage, nor *carried away with pleasure and covetousness, but had ever an *upright mind with him, and would never yield to any wrong

The sharp and cruel conditions of Cassius

Brutus' gentle and fair conditions.

Cf. *Julius Caesar*, IV. iii. 30, 1. [2] *Ibid.* IV. iii. 43, 4.

or injustice, the which was the chiefest cause of his fame, of*
his rising, and of the good will that every man bare him : for*
they were all persuaded that his intent was good.[1]*
For they did not certainly believe, that if Pompey
himself had overcome Caesar he would have re-
signed his authority to the law : but rather they
were of opinion that he would still keep the sovereignty and
absolute government in his hands, taking only, to please the
people, the title of Consul or Dictator, or of some other more
civil office. And as for Cassius, a hot, choleric, and cruel
man, that would oftentimes be carried away from justice for
gain : it was certainly thought that he made war, and put
himself into sundry dangers, more to have absolute power
and authority, than to defend the liberty of his country.
For they that will also consider others, that were elder men
than they, as Cinna, Marius, and Carbo, it is out of doubt
that the end and hope of their victory was to be Lords of
their country : and in manner they did all confess that they
fought for the tyranny, and to be Lords of the Empire of
Rome. And in contrary manner, his enemies themselves did
never reprove Brutus for any such change or desire.
For it was said that Antonius spake it openly*
divers times, that he thought that of all them that*
had slain Caesar there was none but Brutus only, that*
was moved to do it as thinking the act commendable of it-*
self; but that all the other conspirators did conspire his†

Marginal notes:
- Brutus' intent good, if he had overcome.
- Antonius' testimony of Brutus.

[1] Cf. *Julius Caesar*, V. v. 73–5.

MARCUS BRUTUS 153

†death for some private malice or envy, that they otherwise †did bear unto him.[1] Hereby it appeareth that Brutus did not trust so much to the power of his army, as he did to his own virtue : as is to be seen by his writings. For approaching near to the instant danger, he wrote unto Pomponius Atticus, that his affairs had the best hap that could be. 'For,' said he, 'either I will set my country at liberty by battle, or by honourable death rid me of this bondage.' And furthermore, that they being certain and assured of all things else, this one thing only was doubtful to them whether they should live or die with liberty. He wrote also that Antonius had his due payment for his folly. For where he might have been a partner equally of the glory of Brutus, Cassius and Cato, and have made one with them, he liked better to choose to be joined with Octavius Caesar alone : 'with whom, though now he be not overcome by us, yet shall he shortly after also have war with him.' And truly he proved a true Prophet, for so came it indeed to pass. *Now, whilst Brutus and Cassius were together in *the city of Smyrna, Brutus prayed Cassius to let him have *some part of his money, whereof he had great store, because *all that he could rap and rend of his side he had bestowed *it in making so great a number of ships, that by means of *them they should keep all the sea at their commandment. *Cassius' friends hindered this request, and earnestly dis-

Brutus' noble mind to his country

Brutus a true Prophet of Antonius.

[1] Ct. *Julius Caesar*, V. v. 68-72

suaded him from it: persuading him, that it was no reason*
that Brutus should have the money which Cassius had*
gotten together by sparing, and levied with great evil will of*
the people their subjects, for him to bestow liberally upon*
his soldiers, and by this means to win their good wills by*
Cassius' charge. This notwithstanding, Cassius gave him*
the third part of his total sum.[1] So Cassius and Brutus*

Cassius wan the city of Rhodes. then departing from each other, Cassius took the city of Rhodes, where he too dishonestly and cruelly used himself: although when he came into the city, he answered some of the inhabitants, who called him Lord and King, that he was neither Lord nor King, but he only that had slain him, that would have been Lord and King. Brutus, departing from thence, sent unto the Lycians to require money, and men of war. But there was a certain Orator called Naucrates, that made the cities to rebel against him, insomuch that the countrymen of that country kept the straits and little mountains, thinking by that means to stop Brutus' passage. Wherefore

Brutus' gests in Lycia. Brutus sent his horsemen against them, who stale upon them as they were at dinner, and slew six hundred of them: and taking all the small towns and villages, he did let all the prisoners he took go without payment of ransom, hoping, by this his great courtesy to win them, to draw all the rest of the country unto him. But they were so fierce and obstinate, that they would

[1] Cf. *Julius Caesar*, IV. iii. 69–84.

mutiny for every small hurt they received as they passed by their country, and did despise his courtesy and good nature : until that at length he went to besiege the city of the Xanthians, within the which were shut up the cruellest and most warlikest men of Lycia. There was a river that ran by the walls of the city, in the which many men saved themselves, swimming between two waters, and fled : howbeit they laid nets overthwart the river, and tied little bells on the top of them, to sound when any man was taken in the nets. The Xanthians made a sally out by night, and came to fire certain engines of battery that beat down their walls : but they were presently driven in again by the Romans, so soon as they were discovered. The wind by chance was marvellous big, and increased the flame so sore, that it violently carried it into the cranews of the wall of the city, so that the next houses unto them were straight set a fire thereby. Wherefore Brutus being afraid that all the city would take of a fire, he presently commanded his men to quench the fire, and to save the town if it might be. But the Lycians at that instant fell into such a frenzy and strange and horrible despair, that no man can well express it : and a man can not more rightly compare or liken it, than to a frantic and most desperate desire to die. For all of them together, with their wives and children, Masters and servants, and of all sorts of age whatsoever, fought upon the ramper of their walls, and did cast down stones

The city of Xanthus set a fire

The desperate end of the Xanthians

and fireworks on the Romans, which were very busy in quenching the flame of the fire to save the city. And in contrary manner also, they brought faggots, dry wood, and reeds, to bring the fire further into the city as much as might be, increasing it by such things as they brought. Now when the fire had gotten into all the parts of the city, and that the flame burnt bright in every place: Brutus, being sorry to see it, got upon his horse, and rode round about the walls of the city, to see if it were possible to save it, and held up his hands to the inhabitants, praying them to pardon their city, and to save themselves. Howbeit they would not be persuaded, but did all that they could possible to cast themselves away, not only men and women, but also little children. For some of them weeping and crying out did cast themselves into the fire: others headlong throwing themselves down from the walls brake their necks: others also made their necks bare to the naked swords of their fathers, and undid their clothes, praying them to kill them with their own hands. After the city was burnt, they found a woman hanged up by her neck, holding one of her children in her hand dead by her, hanged up also: and in the other hand a burning torch setting fire on her house. Some would have had Brutus to have seen her, but he would not see so horrible and tragical a sight: but when he heard it he fell a weeping, and caused a Herald to make proclamation by sound of trumpet, that he would give a certain sum of money to every soldier that could save a Xanthian. So there were not (as it is reported) above fifty of them saved, and yet they were saved against their wills. Thus the Xanthians having ended the revolution of their fatal destiny, after a long continuance of time they did through their desperation renew the memory of the lamentable calamities of their Ancestors. Who in like manner, in the wars of the Persians, did burn their city, and destroyed themselves. Therefore Brutus likewise besieging the city of the Patareans, perceiving that they stoutly resisted him, he was also afraid of that, and could not well tell whether he should give assault to it or not, lest they would fall into the despair and desperation of the Xanthians. Howbeit, having taken certain of their women prisoners, he sent them back again without payment of ransom. Now they that were the wives and Daughters of the noblest men of the city, reporting unto their parents that they had found Brutus a merciful, just, and courteous man : they persuaded them to yield themselves and their city unto him, the which they did. So, after they had thus yielded themselves, divers other cities also followed them, and did the like : and found Brutus more merciful and courteous than they thought they should have done, but specially far above Cassius. For Cassius, about the self same time, after he had compelled the Rhodians every man to deliver all the ready money they had in gold and silver in their houses, the which being brought together

The Patareans do yield themselves unto Brutus

The extreme covetousness and cruelty of Cassius to the Rhodians

amounted to the sum of eight thousand talents: yet he condemned the city besides to pay the sum of five hundred talents more. Where Brutus in contrary manner, after he had levied of all the country of Lycia but a hundred and fifty talents only, he departed thence into the country of Ionia, and did them no more hurt. Now Brutus in all this journey did many notable acts and worthy of memory, both for rewarding, as also in punishing those that had deserved it: wherefore among the rest I will tell you of one thing, of the which he himself and all the noblemen of the Romans were marvellous glad. When Pompey the great (having lost the battle against Julius Caesar in the fields of Pharsalia) came and fell upon the coast of Egypt, hard by the city of Pelusium, those that were protectors to the young king Ptolemy, being then but a child, sate in council with his servants and friends, what they should determine in that case. They were not all of one mind in this consultation: for some thought it good to receive Pompey, others also, that they should drive him out of Egypt. But there was a certain Rhetorician called Theodotus, that was born in the Isle of Chio, who was the king's Schoolmaster to teach him Rhetoric. He, being called to this council for lack of sufficienter men, said, that both the one and the other side went awry, as well those that were of opinion to receive Pompey, as the other that would have had him driven

Brutus' clemency unto the Lycians.

Theodotus born in Chio, a Rhetorician Schoolmaster to Ptolemy the young king of Egypt.

MARCUS BRUTUS

away: and that the best way was (considering the present time) that they should lay hold on him, and kill him, adding withal this sentence, that 'a dead man biteth not.' The whole council stuck to this opinion. So, for a notable example of incredible misfortune, and unlooked for unto Pompey, Pompey the great was slain, by the motion and council of this wicked Rhetorician Theodotus, as Theodotus afterwards did himself boast of it. But when Julius Caesar came afterwards into Egypt, the wicked men that consented to this counsel had their payment according to their deserts: for they died every man of them a wicked death, saving this Theodotus, whom fortune respited a little while lenger, and yet in that time he lived a poor and miserable life, never tarrying long in any one place. So, Brutus going up and down Asia, Theodotus could hide himself no lenger, but was brought unto Brutus, where he suffered pains of death: so that he wan more fame by his *death, than ever he did in his life. About that *time, Brutus sent to pray Cassius to come to the *city of Sardis, and so he did. Brutus, understand- *ing of his coming, went to meet him with all his *friends.[1] There, both their armies being armed, *they called them both Emperors. Now, as it *commonly happeneth in great affairs between two *persons, both of them having many friends and so many

> Theodotus' saying. 'A dead man biteth not.'

> Theodotus Chian the Rhetorician that gave counsel to kill Pompey, was put to death by Brutus

> Brutus and Cassius do meet at the city of Sardis.

[1] Cf. *Julius Caesar*, IV. ii.

Captains under them, there ran tales and complaints betwixt them. Therefore, before they fell in hand with any
other matter, they went into a little chamber together, and
bade every man avoid, and did shut the doors to them.
Then they began to pour out their complaints one
to the other, and grew hot and loud, earnestly
accusing one another, and at length fell both
a-weeping.[1] Their friends that were without the
chamber hearing them loud within, and angry between
themselves, they were both amazed, and afraid also lest it
would grow to further matter: but yet they were commanded, that no man should come to them.[2] Notwithstanding, one Marcus Favonius, that had been a
friend and follower of Cato while he lived, and
took upon him to counterfeit a Philosopher, not
with wisdom and discretion, but with a certain bedlam and
frantic motion: he would needs come into the chamber,
though the men offered to keep him out. But it was no
boot to let Favonius, when a mad mood or toy took him
in the head: for he was a hot hasty man, and sudden in
all his doings, and cared for never a Senator of
them all. Now, though he used this bold manner
of speech after the profession of the Cynic Philosophers (as who would say, dogs), yet this boldness
did no hurt many times, because they did but laugh at
him to see him so mad. This Favonius at that time, in

[1] Cf. *Julius Caesar*, IV. iii. 1–122.   [2] *Ibid.* IV. ii. 50, 1.

MARCUS BRUTUS

*despite of the doorkeepers, came into the chamber, and
*with a certain scoffing and mocking gesture which he
*counterfeited of purpose, he rehearsed the verses which old
*Nestor said in Homer :

*My lords, I pray you hearken both to me,
†For I have seen moe years than suchie three.

*Cassius fell a-laughing at him : but Brutus thrust him out
*of the chamber, and called him dog, and counterfeit Cynic.[1]
Howbeit his coming in brake their strife at that time, and
so they left each other. The self same night Cassius prepared
his supper in his chamber, and Brutus brought his friends
with him. So, when they were set at supper, Favonius
came to sit down after he had washed. Brutus told him
aloud, no man sent for him, and bade them set him at the
upper end, meaning indeed at the lower end of the bed.
Favonius made no ceremony, but thrust in amongst the midst
of them, and made all the company laugh at him : so they
were merry all suppertime, and full of their Philosophy.
*The next day after, Brutus, upon complaint of the Sardians,
†did condemn and noted Lucius Pella for a defamed person,[2]
that had been a Praetor of the Romans, and whom Brutus
*had given charge unto : for that he was accused and con-
*victed of robbery and pilfery in his office. This judgement
*much misliked Cassius :[2] because he himself had secretly
(not many days before) warned two of his friends, attainted

[1] Cf. *Julius Caesar*, IV. iii. 123-137. [2] *Ibid.* IV. iii. 2, 3.
VOL. I. M

and convicted of the like offences, and openly had cleared them : but yet he did not therefore leave to employ them in any manner of service as he did before. And therefore he greatly reproved Brutus, for that he would shew himself* so straight and severe, in such a time as was meeter to bear* a little, than to take things at the worst. Brutus in contrary* manner answered, that he should remember the* Ides of March, at which time they slew Julius† Caesar : who neither pilled nor polled the country,† but only was a favourer and suborner of all them† that did rob and spoil by his countenance and authority.[1]* And if there were any occasion whereby they might honestly set aside justice and equity, they should have had more reason to have suffered Caesar's friends to have robbed and done what wrong and injury they had would, than to bear with their own men. For then, said he, they could but have said they had been cowards : and now they may accuse us of injustice, beside the pains we take, and the danger we put ourselves into. And thus may we see what Brutus' intent and purpose was. But as they both prepared to pass over again out of Asia into Europe, there went a rumour that there appeared a wonderful sign unto him. Brutus was a careful man, and slept very little, both for that his diet was moderate, as also because he was continually occupied. He never slept in the day time, and in the night no lenger than the time he was

Julius Caesar slain at the Ides of March.

The wonderful constancy of Brutus in matters of justice and equity.

[1] Cf. *Julius Caesar*, IV. iii. 7–26.

MARCUS BRUTUS

driven to be alone, and when everybody else took their rest. But now whilst he was in war, and his head ever busily occupied to think of his affairs, and what would happen: after he had slumbered a little after supper, he spent all the rest of the night in despatching of his weightiest causes, and after he had taken *order for them, if he had any leisure left him, he would *read some book till the third watch of the night,[1] at what time the Captains, petty Captains, and Colonels did use to come unto him. So, being ready to go into Europe, one night very late (when all the camp took quiet rest) as he †was in his tent with a little light, thinking of weighty †matters: he thought he heard one come in to him, †and casting his eye towards the door of his tent, †that he saw a wonderful strange and monstrous †shape of a body coming towards him, and said †never a word. So Brutus boldly asked what he was, a god †or a man, and what cause brought him thither. The spirit †answered him, 'I am thy evil spirit, Brutus: and thou †shalt see me by the city of Philippi.' Brutus, being no †otherwise afraid, replied again unto it: 'Well, then I shall ┤see thee again.' The spirit presently vanished away, and †Brutus called his men unto him, who told him that they †heard no noise, nor saw anything at all.[2] Thereupon Brutus returned again to think on his matters as he did

<small>Brutus' care and watching.</small>

<small>A spirit appeared unto Brutus in the city of Sardis.</small>

[1] Cf. *Julius Caesar*, IV. iii. 251.
[2] *Ibid.* IV. iii. 274–303; *Life of Caesar*, p. 107.

before : and when the day brake, he went unto Cassius, to
tell him what vision had appeared unto him in the night.
Cassius being in opinion an Epicurean,[1] and reasoning

Cassius' opinion of spirits, after the Epicureans' sect. thereon with Brutus, spake to him touching the vision thus. 'In our sect, Brutus, we have an opinion, that we do not always feel or see that which we suppose we do both see and feel : but that our
senses being credulous, and therefore easily abused (when
they are idle and unoccupied in their own objects), are
induced to imagine they see and conjecture that which they
in truth do not. For our mind is quick and cunning to
work (without either cause or matter) anything in the
imagination whatsoever. And therefore the imagination
is resembled to clay, and the mind to the potter : who
without any other cause than his fancy and pleasure,
changeth it into what fashion and form he will. And this
The cause of dreams. doth the diversity of our dreams shew unto us.
For our imagination doth upon a small fancy grow
from conceit to conceit, altering both in passions and forms
of things imagined. For the mind of man is ever occupied,
and that continual moving is nothing but an imagination.
But yet there is a further cause of this in you. For you
being by nature given to melancholic discoursing, and of late
continually occupied, your wits and senses having been
overlaboured do easilier yield to such imaginations. For,
to say that there are spirits or angels, and if there were, that

[1] Cf. *Julius Caesar*, V, 1. 76, 7 , *Life of Cæsar*, p. 100

they had the shape of men, or such voices, or any power at all to come unto us : it is a mockery. And for mine own part I would there were such, because that we should not only have soldiers, horses, and ships, but also the aid of the gods, to guide and further our honest and honourable attempts.' With these words Cassius did somewhat comfort and quiet Brutus. When they raised their camp, †there came two Eagles that flying with a marvel†lous force lighted upon two of the foremost ensigns, †and always followed the soldiers, which gave them meat, †and fed them, until they came near to the city of Philippi : †and there, one day only before the battle, they both flew †away.[1] Now Brutus had conquered the most part of all the people and nations of that country : but if there were any other city or Captain to overcome, then they made all clear before them, and so drew towards the coasts of Thassos. There Norbanus lying in camp in a certain place called the straits, by another place called Symbolon (which is a port of the sea), Cassius and Brutus compassed him in in such sort, that he was driven to forsake the place which was of great strength for him, and he was also in danger beside to have lost all his army. For Octavius Caesar could not follow him because of his sickness, and therefore stayed behind : whereupon they had taken his army, had not Antonius' aid been, which made such wonderful speed, that Brutus could scant believe it. So Caesar came not thither of ten days

A wonderful sign by two Eagles.

[1] Cf. *Julius Caesar*, V. i. 80–4.

after: and Antonius camped against Cassius, and Brutus on th' other side against Caesar. The Romans called the valley between both camps, the Philippian fields: and there were never seen two so great armies of the Romans, one before the other, ready to fight. In truth, Brutus' army was inferior to Octavius Caesar's, in number of men: but for bravery and rich furniture, Brutus' army far excelled Caesar's. For the most part of their armours were silver and gilt, which Brutus had bountifully given them: although in all other things he taught his Captains to live in order without excess. But for the bravery of armour and weapon, which soldiers should carry in their hands, or otherwise wear upon their backs: he thought that it was an encouragement unto them that by nature are greedy of honour, and that it maketh them also fight like devils, that love to get, and be afraid to lose: because they fight to keep their armour and weapon, as also their goods and lands. Now, when they came to muster their armies, Octavius Caesar took the muster of his army within the trenches of his camp, and gave his men only a little corn, and five silver Drachmas to every man to sacrifice to the gods, and to pray for victory. But Brutus, scorning this misery and niggardliness, first of all mustered his army, and did purify it in the fields, according to the

[margin: Brutus' and Cassius' camps before the city of Philippi against Octavius Caesar and Antonius.]

[margin: Brutus' soldiers bravely armed.]

[margin: Brutus' opinion for the bravery of soldiers in their armour and weapons.]

manner of the Romans: and then he gave unto every band a number of wethers to sacrifice, and fifty silver Drachmas to every soldier. So that Brutus' and Cassius' soldiers were better pleased, and more courageously bent to fight at the day of the battle, than their enemies' soldiers were. Notwithstanding, being busily occupied about the ceremonies of this purification, it is reported that there chanced certain unlucky signs unto Cassius. For one of his Sergeants that carried the rods before him brought him the garland of flowers turned backwards, the which he should have worn on his head in the time of sacrificing. Moreover it is reported also that at another time before, in certain sports and triumph where they carried an image of Cassius' victory of clean gold, it fell by chance, the man stumbling that carried it. And yet further, there were seen a marvellous number of fowls of prey, that feed upon dead carcases: and beehives also were found, where bees were gathered together in a certain place within the trenches of the camp: the which place the Soothsayers thought good to shut out of the precinct of the camp, for to take away the superstitious fear and mistrust men would have
*of it. The which began somewhat to alter Cassius'
*mind from Epicurus' opinions,[1] and had put the
*soldiers also in a marvellous fear. Thereupon
*Cassius was of opinion not to try this war at
*one battle, but rather to delay time, and to draw it

Side notes: Unlucky signs unto Cassius. Cassius' and Brutus' opinions about battle.

[1] Cf. *Julius Caesar*, V. i. 78, 9.

out in length, considering that they were the stronger in*
money, and the weaker in men and armours. But Brutus in*
contrary manner did alway before, and at that time also,*
desire nothing more, than to put all to the hazard of battle*
as soon as might be possible [1] : to the end he might either*
quickly restore his country to her former liberty, or rid him
forthwith of this miserable world, being still troubled in
following and maintaining of such great armies together.
But, perceiving that in the daily skirmishes and bickerings
they made, his men were alway the stronger, and ever had
the better: that yet quickened his spirits again, and did put
him in better heart. And furthermore, because that some*
of their own men had already yielded themselves to their*
enemies, and that it was suspected moreover divers others*
would do the like:[1] that made many of Cassius' friends,*
which were of his mind before, (when it came to be debated
in council whether the battle should be fought or not), that
they were then of Brutus' mind. But yet was there one of
Brutus' friends called Atellius, that was against it,
and was of opinion that they should tarry the next
winter. Brutus asked him what he should get by
tarrying a year lenger? 'If I get nought else,' quoth
Atellius again, 'yet have I lived so much lenger.' Cassius
was very angry with this answer: and Atellius was maliced
and esteemed the worse for it of all men. Thereupon it
was presently determined they should fight battle the next

Atellius' opinion for the battle.

[1] Cf *Julius Caesar*, IV. iii. 197-223.

day. So Brutus all suppertime looked with a cheerful countenance, like a man that had good hope, and talked very wisely of Philosophy, and after supper went to bed. But touching Cassius, Messala reporteth that he supped by himself in his tent with a few of his friends, and that all suppertime he looked very sadly, and was full of thoughts, although it was against his nature: and that after supper *he took him by the hand, and holding him fast (in *token of kindness as his manner was) told him in *Greek: 'Messala, I protest unto thee, and make †thee my witness, that I am compelled against my †mind and will (as Pompey the great was) to jeo- †pard the liberty of our country to the hazard of †a battle.[1] And yet we must be lively, and of good courage, considering our good fortune, whom we should wrong too much to mistrust her, although we follow evil counsel.' Messala writeth, that Cassius having spoken these last words unto him, he bade him farewell, and willed him to come to supper to him the next night following, *because it was his birthday.[2] The next morning, by break of day, the signal of battle was set out in Brutus' and Cassius' camp, which was an arming scarlet coat: and both the Chieftains spake together in the midst of their armies. There Cassius began to speak †first, and said: 'The gods grant us, O Brutus, that †this day we may win the field, and ever after to live all the

Cassius' words unto Messala the night before the battle.

Brutus and Cassius talk before the battle.

[1] Cf. *Julius Caesar*, V. i. 73–6. [2] *Ibid.* V. i. 72, 3; iii. 23, 4.

rest of our life quietly, one with another. But sith the
gods have so ordained it, that the greatest and chiefest
things amongst men are most uncertain, and that if the battle
fall out otherwise to-day than we wish or look for, we shall
hardly meet again: what art thou then determined to do,
to fly, or die?'[1] Brutus answered him, 'Being
yet but a young man, and not over greatly experi-
enced in the world, I trust (I know not how) a
certain rule of Philosophy, by the which I did greatly blame
and reprove Cato for killing of himself, as being no lawful
nor godly act, touching the gods, nor, concerning men,
valiant; not to give place and yield to divine providence,
and not constantly and patiently to take whatsoever it
pleaseth him to send us, but to draw back and fly[2] but,
being now in the midst of the danger, I am of a contrary
mind. For if it be not the will of God that this battle fall
out fortunate for us, I will look no more for hope, neither
seek to make any new supply for war again, but will rid me
of this miserable world, and content me with my fortune.
For I gave up my life for my country in the Ides of March,
for the which I shall live in another more glorious world.'[3]
Cassius fell a-laughing to hear what he said, and embracing
him, 'Come on then,' said he, 'let us go and charge our
enemies with this mind. For either we shall conquer, or we
shall not need to fear the Conquerors.' After this talk,

Brutus' answer to Cassius.

[1] Cf. *Julius Caesar*, V. i. 93-100.   [2] *Ibid.* V. i. 101-8.
[3] *Ibid.* V. i. 113-14.

MARCUS BRUTUS

they fell to consultation among their friends for the ordering of the battle. Then Brutus prayed Cassius he might have the leading of the right wing, the which men thought was far meeter for Cassius: both because he was the elder man, and also for that he had the better experience. But yet Cassius gave it him, and willed that Messala (who had charge of one of the warlikest legions they had) should be also in that wing with Brutus. So Brutus presently sent out his horsemen, who were excellently well appointed, and his footmen also were as willing and ready to give charge. Now Antonius' men did cast a trench from the marish by the which they lay, to cut off Cassius' way to come to the sea: and Caesar, at the least his army, stirred not. As for Octavius Caesar himself, he *was not in his camp, because he was sick. And for his peo-*ple, they little thought the enemies would have given them *battle,[1] but only have made some light skirmishes to hinder them that wrought in the trench, and with their darts and slings, to have kept them from finishing of their work: but they, taking no heed to them that came full upon them to give them battle, marvelled much at the great noise they heard, that came from the place where they were casting *their trench. In the meantime Brutus, that led the right *wing, sent little bills to the Colonels and Captains of private *bands, in the which he wrote the word of the battle;[2] and he himself, riding a-horseback by all the troops, did speak to

The battle at Philippi against Octavius Caesar and Antonius.

[1] Cf. *Julius Caesar,* V. i. 2, 3.   [2] *Ibid.* V. ii. 1, 2.

them, and encouraged them to stick to it like men. So by
this means very few of them understood what was the word
of the battle, and, besides, the most part of them never tarried to have it told them, but ran with great fury to assail
the enemies · whereby, through this disorder, the legions
were marvellously scattered and dispersed one from the
other. For first of all, Messala's legion, and then the next
unto them, went beyond the left wing of the enemies, and
did nothing, but glancing by them overthrew some as they
went, and so going on further fell right upon Caesar's camp
out of the which (as himself writeth in his commentaries),
he had been conveyed away a little before, through the
counsel and advice of one of his friends called Marcus
Artorius : who, dreaming in the night, had a vision appeared
unto him, that commanded Octavius Caesar should be carried out of his camp. Insomuch as it was thought he was
slain, because his litter (which had nothing in it) was thrust
through and through with pikes and darts. There was great
slaughter in this camp. For amongst others there were
slain two thousand Lacedaemonians, who were arrived but
even a little before, coming to aid Caesar. The other also
that had not glanced by, but had given a charge full upon
Caesar's battle, they easily made them fly, because they were
greatly troubled for the loss of their camp, and of them
there were slain by hand three legions. Then, being very
earnest to follow the chase of them that fled, they ran in
amongst them hand over head into their camp, and Brutus

among them. But that which the conquerors thought not of, occasion shewed it unto them that were overcome and that was the left wing of their enemies left naked, and unguarded of them of the right wing, who were strayed too far off, in following of them that were overthrown. So they gave a hot charge upon them. But notwithstanding all the force they made, they could not break into the midst of their battle, where they found men that received them and valiantly made head against them. Howbeit they brake and overthrew the left wing where Cassius was, by reason of the great disorder among them, and also because they had no intelligence how the right wing had sped. So they chased them, beating them into their camp, the which they spoiled, none of both the Chieftains being present there. For Antonius, as it is reported, to fly the fury of the first charge, was gotten into the next marish · and no man could tell what became of Octavius Caesar, after he was carried out of his camp. Insomuch that there were certain soldiers that shewed their swords bloodied, and said that they had slain him, and did describe his face, and shewed what age he was of. Furthermore, the voward and the midst of Brutus' battle had already put all their enemies to flight that withstood them, with great slaughter: so that Brutus had conquered all of his side, and Cassius had lost all on the other side. For nothing undid them, but that Brutus went not to help Cassius, thinking he had

Octavius Caesar falsely reported to be slain at the battle of Philippi

Cassius' misfortune

overcome them, as himself had done : and Cassius on the other side tarried not for Brutus, thinking he had been overthrown, as himself was. And to prove that the victory fell on Brutus' side, Messala confirmeth it, that they wan three eagles, and divers other ensigns of their enemies, and their enemies wan never a one of theirs. Now Brutus returning from the chase, after he had slain and sacked Caesar's men, he wondered much that he could not see Cassius' tent standing up high as it was wont, neither the other tents of his camp standing as they were before, because all the whole camp had been spoiled, and the tents thrown down, at the first coming in of the enemies. But they that were about Brutus, whose sight served them better, told him that they saw a great glistering of harness, and a number of silvered targets, that went and came into Cassius' camp, and were not (as they took it) the armours nor the number of men that they had left there to guard the camp : and yet that they saw not such a number of dead bodies, and great overthrow, as there should have been if so many legions had been slain.

<small>Cassius offended with the sundry errors Brutus and his men committed in battle.</small> This made Brutus at the first mistrust that which had happened. So he appointed a number of men to keep the camp of his enemy which he had taken, and caused his men to be sent for that yet followed the chase, and gathered them together, thinking to lead them to aid Cassius, who was in this state as you shall hear. First of all he was marvellous angry to*

*see how Brutus' men ran to give charge upon their
*enemies, and tarried not for the word of the battle
*nor commandment to give charge, and it grieved him
*beside, that after he had overcome them, his men fell
*straight to spoil, and were not careful to compass in the rest
*of the enemies behind. But with tarrying too long also,
*more than through the valiantness or foresight of the
*Captains his enemies, Cassius found himself compassed in
*with the right wing of his enemies' army.[1] Whereupon
his horsemen brake immediately, and fled for life towards
*the sea. Furthermore, perceiving his footmen to give
*ground, he did what he could to keep them from flying,
*and took an ensign from one of the ensign-bearers that fled,
*and stuck it fast at his feet: [2] although with much
ado he could scant keep his own guard together. <small>Cassius' valiantness in wars</small>
*So Cassius himself was at length compelled to fly
*with a few about him, unto a little hill, from whence
*they might easily see what was done in all the plain [3]:
*howbeit Cassius himself saw nothing, for his sight was
*very bad,[4] saving that he saw (and yet with much ado)
*how the enemies spoiled his camp before his eyes.[3]
He saw also a great troop of horsemen whom Brutus
sent to aid him, and thought that they were his
*enemies that followed him: but yet he sent Titinius, one
*of them that was with him, to go and know what they were.

[1] Cf. *Julius Caesar*, V. iii. 5-8. [2] *Ibid.* V. iii. 1-4.
[3] *Ibid.* V. iii. 9-14. [4] *Ibid.* V. iii. 21.

Brutus' horsemen saw him coming afar off, whom when they knew that he was one of Cassius' chiefest friends, they shouted out for joy: and they that were familiarly acquainted with him lighted from their horses, and went and embraced him. The rest compassed him in round about a-horseback, with songs of victory and great rushing of their harness, so that they made all the field ring again for joy.

<small>The importance of error and mistaking in wars.</small> But this marred all. For Cassius thinking indeed that Titinius was taken of the enemies,[1] he then spake these words: 'Desiring too much to live, I have lived to see one of my best friends taken, for my sake, before my face.'[2] After that, he got into a tent where nobody was, and took Pindarus with him, one of his freed bondmen, whom he reserved ever for such a pinch, since the cursed battle of the Parthians where Crassus was slain, though he notwithstanding scaped from that overthrow: but then casting his cloak over his head, <small>Cassius slain by his man Pindarus.</small> and holding out his bare neck unto Pindarus, he gave him his head to be stricken off.[3] So the head was found severed from the body: but after that time Pindarus was never seen more. Whereupon, some took occasion to say that he had slain his master without his commandment. By and by they knew the horsemen that came towards them, and might see Titinius crowned with a garland of triumph, who came

---

[1] Cf. *Julius Caesar*, V. iii. 14-22, 25-32, 81-4.
[2] *Ibid.* V. iii. 34, 5.   [3] *Ibid.* V. iii. 36-40, 43-50.

MARCUS BRUTUS

*before with great speed unto Cassius. But, when he per-
*ceived, by the cries and tears of his friends which tormented
*themselves, the misfortune that had chanced to his Captain
*Cassius by mistaking : he drew out his sword, cursing him-
*self a thousand times that he had tarried so long, The death
*and so slew himself presently in the field.[1] Brutus of Titinius
in the meantime came forward still, and understood also
that Cassius had been overthrown : but he knew nothing of
his death till he came very near to his camp. So when he
*was come thither, after he had lamented the death of Cassius,
†calling him the last of all the Romans, being unpossible that
†Rome should ever breed again so noble and valiant a man
†as he[2] : he caused his body to be buried, and sent it to the
*city of Thassos, fearing lest his funerals within the camp
*should cause great disorder.[3] Then he called his soldiers
together, and did encourage them again. And when he saw
that they had lost all their carriage, which they could not
brook well, he promised every man of them two thousand
Drachmas in recompense. After his soldiers had heard his
Oration, they were all of them prettily cheered again, wondering much at his great liberality, and waited upon him
with great cries when he went his way, praising him for
that he only of the four Chieftains was not overcome in
battle. And to speak the truth, his deeds shewed that he
hoped not in vain to be conqueror. For with few legions

[1] Cf. *Julius Caesar*, V. iii. 51–90.   [2] *Ibid*. V. iii. 99–101.
[3] *Ibid*. V. iii. 104–6.

he had slain and driven all them away, that made head against him: and yet if all his people had fought, and that the most of them had not outgone their enemies to run to spoil their goods, surely it was like enough he had slain them all, and had left never a man of them alive. There were slain of Brutus' side about eight thousand men, counting the soldiers' slaves, whom Brutus called *Brigas*: and of the enemies' side, as Messala writeth, there were slain, as he supposeth, more than twice as many moe. Wherefore they were more discouraged than Brutus, until that very late at night there was one of Cassius' men called Demetrius who went unto Antonius, and carried his master's clothes, whereof he was stripped not long before, and his sword also. This encouraged Brutus' enemies, and made them so brave, that the next morning betimes they stood in battle ray again before Brutus. But, on Brutus' side, both his camps stood wavering, and that in great danger. For his own camp, being full of prisoners, required a good guard to look unto them: and Cassius' camp on the other side took the death of their Captain very heavily, and beside, there was some vile grudge between them that were overcome and those that did overcome. For this cause therefore Brutus did set them in battle ray, but yet kept himself from giving battle. Now for the slaves that were prisoners, which were a great number of them, and went and came to and fro amongst the armed men, not without suspicion: he com-

Marginal note: The number of men slain at the battle of Philippi.

manded they should kill them. But for the freemen, he
sent them freely home, and said, that they were better
prisoners with his enemies, than with him. For Brutus'
with them they were slaves and servants: and clemency
with him they were free men and citizens. So, courtesy.
when he saw that divers Captains and his friends did so
cruelly hate some, that they would by no means save their
lives: Brutus himself hid them, and secretly sent them away.
Among these prisoners, there was one Volumnius a jester,
and Sacculio a common player, of whom Brutus made no
accompt at all. Howbeit his friends brought them unto
him, and did accuse them, that though they were prisoners,
they did not let to laugh them to scorn, and to jest broadly
with them. Brutus made no answer to it, because his head
was occupied other ways. Whereupon Messala Corvinus
said, that it were good to whip them on a scaffold, and
then to send them naked, well whipped, unto the Captains
of their enemies, to shew them their shame, to keep such
mates as those in their camp, to play the fools, to make
them sport. Some that stood by laughed at his device.
But Publius Casca, that gave Julius Caesar the first wound
when he was slain, said then: 'It doth not become us to
be thus merry at Cassius' funerals: and for thee, Brutus,
thou shalt show what estimation thou madest of such a
Captain thy compeer, by putting to death, or saving the
lives of these bloods, who hereafter will mock him, and
defame his memory.' Brutus answered again in choler:

'Why then do you come to tell me of it, Casca, and do not yourselves what you think good?' When they heard him say so, they took his answer for a consent against these poor unfortunate men, to suffer them to do what they thought good: and therefore they carried them away, and slew them. Afterwards Brutus performed the promise he had made to the soldiers, and gave them the two thousand Drachmas apiece, but yet he first reproved them, because they went and gave charge upon the enemies at the first battle, before they had the word of battle given them: and made them a new promise also, that if in the second battle they fought like men, he would give them the sack and spoil of two cities, to wit, Thessalonica and Lacedaemon.

<small>Brutus' fault wisely excused by Plutarch</small> In all Brutus' life there is but this only fault to be found, and that is not to be gainsaid: though Antonius and Octavius Caesar did reward their soldiers far worse for their victory. For when they had driven all the natural Italians out of Italy, they gave their soldiers their lands and towns, to the which they had no right: and moreover, the only mark they shot at in all this war they made was but to overcome, and reign. Where in contrary manner they had so great an opinion of Brutus' virtue, that the common voice and opinion of the world would not suffer him neither to overcome, nor to save himself otherwise than justly and honestly, and specially after Cassius' death: whom men burdened, that oftentimes he moved Brutus to great cruelty. But now, like as

the mariners on the sea after the rudder of their ship is broken by tempest, do seek to nail on some other piece of wood in lieu thereof, and do help themselves to keep them from hurt as much as may be upon that instant danger: even so Brutus having such a great army to govern, and his affairs standing very tickle, and having no other Captain coequal with him in dignity and authority: he was forced to employ them he had, and likewise to be ruled by them in many things, and was of mind himself also to grant them anything, that he thought might make them serve like noble soldiers at time of need. For Cassius' soldiers were very evil to be ruled, and did shew themselves very stubborn and lusty in the camp, because they had no Chieftain that did command them: but yet rank cowards to their enemies, because they had once overcome them. On the other side Octavius Caesar and Antonius were not in much better state: for first of all, they lacked victuals. And because they were lodged in low places, they looked to abide a hard and sharp winter, being camped as they were by the marish side, and also for that after the battle there had fallen plenty of rain about the autumn, where through all their tents were full of mire and dirt, the which by reason of the cold did freeze incontinently. But beside all these discommodities, there came news unto them of the great loss they had of their men by sea. For Brutus' ships met with a great aid and supply of men, which were sent them out of Italy, and they overthrew them in such

Brutus' victory by sea.

sort, that there scaped but few of them: and yet they were so famished, that they were compelled to eat the tackle and sails of their ships. Thereupon they were very desirous to fight a battle again, before Brutus should have intelligence of this good news for him: for it chanced so, that the battle was fought by sea on the self same day it was fought by land. But by ill fortune, rather than through the malice or negligence of the Captains, this victory came not to Brutus' ear till twenty days after. For had he known of it before, he would not have been brought to have fought a second battle, considering that he had excellent good provision for his army for a long time, and, besides, lay in a place of great strength, so as his camp could not be greatly hurt by the winter, nor also distressed by his enemies: and further, he had been a quiet Lord, being a conqueror by sea, as he was also by land. This would have marvellously encouraged him. Howbeit the state of Rome (in my opinion) being now brought to that pass, that it could no more abide to be governed by many Lords, but required one only absolute Governor, God, to prevent Brutus that it should not come to his government, kept this victory from his knowledge, though indeed it came but a little too late. For the day before the last battle was given, very late in the night, came Clodius, one of his enemies, into his camp, who told that Caesar, hearing of the overthrow of his army by sea, desired nothing more than to fight

Wonderful famine among Caesar's soldiers by sea.

The ignorance of Brutus' victory by sea was his utter destruction.

MARCUS BRUTUS 183

a battle before Brutus understood it. Howbeit they gave no credit to his words, but despised him so much that they would not vouchsafe to bring him unto Brutus, because they thought it was but a lie devised, to be the better welcome *for this good news. The self same night, it is *reported that the monstrous spirit, which had *appeared before unto Brutus in the city of Sardis, *did now appear again unto him in the self same *shape and form, and so vanished away, and said never a *word.[1] Now Publius Volumnius, a grave and wise Philosopher, that had been with Brutus from the beginning of this war, he doth make no mention of this spirit, but saith, that the greatest Eagle and ensign was covered over with a swarm of bees, and that there was one of the Captains whose arm suddenly fell a-sweating, that it dropped oil of roses from him, and that they oftentimes went about to dry him, but all would do no good. And that before the battle was fought, there were two Eagles fought between both armies, and all the time they fought there was a marvellous great silence all the valley over, both the armies being one before the other, marking this fight between them : and that in the end the Eagle towards Brutus gave over, and flew away. But this is certain, and a true tale : that when the gate of the camp was open, the first man the standard-bearer met that carried the Eagle was an Ethiopian, whom the soldiers for ill luck

The evil spirit appeared again unto Brutus.

Strange sights before Brutus' second battle

[1] Cf. *Julius Caesar*, V. v. 17-19 ; *Life of Caesar,* p. 107.

mangled with their swords. Now, after that Brutus had brought his army into the field, and had set them in battle ray, directly against the voward of his enemy: he paused a long time, before he gave the signal of battle. For Brutus riding up and down to view the bands and companies, it came in his head to mistrust some of them, besides that some came to tell him so much as he thought. Moreover, he saw his horsemen set forward but faintly, and did not go lustily to give charge: but still stayed to see what the footmen would do. Then suddenly, one of the chiefest Knights he had in all his army, called Camulatius, and that was alway marvellously esteemed of for his valiantness until that time: he came hard by Brutus a-horseback, and rode before his face to yield himself unto his enemies. Brutus was marvellous sorry for it, wherefore, partly for anger, and partly for fear of greater treason and rebellion, he suddenly caused his army to march, being past* three of the clock in the afternoon.[1] So in that place where* he himself fought in person, he had the better, and brake into the left wing of his enemies, which gave him way, through the help of his horsemen that gave charge with his footmen, when they saw the enemies in a maze and afraid. Howbeit the other also on the right wing, when the Captains would have had them to have marched: they were afraid to have been compassed in behind, because they were fewer in number than their enemies, and therefore did

Brutus' second battle

[1] Cf. *Julius Caesar*, V. iii. 108.

spread themselves, and leave the midst of their battle.
Whereby they having weakened themselves, they could not
withstand the force of their enemies, but turned tail straight,
and fled. And those that had put them to flight
came in straight upon it to compass Brutus behind, *Brutus'*
who in the midst of the conflict did all that was *valiantness and great skill*
possible for a skilful Captain and valiant soldier: *in wars.*
both for his wisdom, as also for his hardiness, for the obtaining of victory. But that which wan him the victory at
the first battle did now lose it him at the second. For at
the first time, the enemies that were broken and fled were
straight cut in pieces: but at the second battle, of Cassius'
men that were put to flight, there were few slain: and
they that saved themselves by speed, being afraid because
they had been overcome, did discourage the rest of the army
when they came to join with them, and filled all the army
*with fear and disorder. There was the son of M. *The death*
*Cato slain, valiantly fighting amongst the lusty *of the valiant*
*youths. For, notwithstanding that he was very *young man Cato,*
*weary, and overharried, yet would he not therefore *the son of Marcus*
*fly, but manfully fighting and laying about him, *Cato.*
*telling aloud his name, and also his father's name, at length
*he was beaten down amongst many other dead bodies of
*his enemies, which he had slain round about him.[1] So
there were slain in the field all the chiefest gentlemen and
nobility that were in his army, who valiantly ran into

[1] Cf. *Julius Caesar*, V. iv. 3–6, 9–11.

any danger to save Brutus' life. Amongst them there was
one of Brutus' friends called Lucilius, who seeing
a troop of barbarous men making no reckoning
of all men else they met in their way, but going
all together right against Brutus, he determined
to stay them with the hazard of his life, and, being left
behind, told them that he was Brutus :[1] and, because they
should believe him, he prayed them to bring him to
Antonius, for he said he was afraid of Caesar, and that he
did trust Antonius better. These barbarous men being
very glad of this good hap, and thinking themselves happy
men, they carried him in the night, and sent some before
unto Antonius, to tell him of their coming. He was marvellous glad of it, and went out to meet them that brought
him.[1] Others also understanding of it, that they had
brought Brutus prisoner : they came out of all parts of the
camp to see him, some pitying his hard fortune, and others
saying, that it was not done like himself, so cowardly to
be taken alive of the barbarous people for fear of death.
When they came near together, Antonius stayed awhile,
bethinking himself how he should use Brutus. In the
meantime Lucilius was brought to him, who stoutly with
a bold countenance said, 'Antonius, I dare assure thee
that no enemy hath taken nor shall take Marcus Brutus
alive : and I beseech God keep him from that fortune.
For wheresoever he be found, alive or dead, he will be

The fidelity of Lucilius unto Brutus.

[1] Cf. *Julius Caesar*, V. iv 12-19.

MARCUS BRUTUS

†found like himself.[1] ' And now for myself, I am come unto thee, having deceived these men of arms here, bearing them down that I was Brutus : and do not refuse to suffer any torment thou wilt put me to.' Lucilius' words made them all amazed that heard him. Antonius on the other side, looking upon all them that had brought him, said unto *them : 'My companions, I think ye are sorry you have *failed of your purpose, and that you think this man hath *done you great wrong : but I do assure you, you have *taken a better booty than that you followed.[2] For, instead of an enemy, you have brought me a friend : and for my part, if you had brought me Brutus alive, truly I cannot tell †what I should have done to him For I had rather have †such men my friends as this man here, than enemies.'[3] Then he embraced Lucilius, and at that time delivered him to one of his friends in custody, and Lucilius ever after served him faithfully, even to his death. Now Brutus having passed a little river, walled in on either side with high rocks, and shadowed with great trees, being then dark night, he went no further, but stayed *at the foot of a rock with certain of his Captains and friends *that followed him [4] : and looking up to the firmament that was full of stars, sighing, he rehearsed two verses, of the which Volumnius wrote the one, to this effect .

Brutus flying.

[1] Cf. *Julius Caesar*, V. iv. 20–5.
[2] *Ibid.* V. iv. 26, 27.
[3] *Ibid.* V. iv. 28, 9
[4] *Ibid.* V v. 1.

> Appian meaneth this by Antonius.

> Let not the wight from whom this mischief went
> (O Jove) escape without due punishment

And saith that he had forgotten the other. Within a little while after, naming his friends that he had seen slain in battle before his eyes, he fetched a greater sigh than before: specially when he came to name Labeo and Flavius, of the which the one was his Lieutenant, and the other Captain of the pioneers of his camp. In the meantime, one of the company being athirst, and seeing Brutus athirst also: he ran to the river for water, and brought it in his sallet. At the self same time they heard a noise on the other side of the river. Whereupon Volumnius took Dardanus, Brutus' servant, with him, to see what it was: and, returning straight again, asked if there were any water left. Brutus, smiling gently, told them all was drunk, 'but they shall bring you some more.' Thereupon he sent him again that went for water before, who was in great danger of being taken by the enemies, and hardly scaped, being sore hurt. Furthermore, Brutus thought that there was no great number of men slain in battle, and, to know the truth of it, there* was one called Statilius, that promised to go through his ene-* mies (for otherwise it was impossible to go see their camp),* and from thence if all were well, that he would lift up a torch* light in the air, and then return again with speed to him.* The torch light was lift up as he had promised, for Statilius* went thither. Now Brutus seeing Statilius tarry long*

MARCUS BRUTUS

*after that, and that he came not again, he said : ' If Statilius
*be alive, he will come again.' But his evil fortune
*was such, that as he came back he lighted in his The death of
*enemies hands, and was slain.[1] Now, the night Statilius
*being far spent, Brutus as he sate bowed towards Clitus,
*one of his men, and told him somewhat in his ear : the
*other answered him not, but fell a-weeping. Thereupon
*he proved Dardanus, and said somewhat also to him :[2] at
*length he came to Volumnius himself, and speaking to him
*in Greek, prayed him for the study's sake which brought
*them acquainted together, that he would help him to put
*his hand to his sword, to thrust it in him to kill him.
*Volumnius denied his request,[3] and so did many others :
†and amongst the rest, one of them said, there was no
†tarrying for them there, but that they must needs fly [4]
Then Brutus rising up, ' We must fly indeed,' said he,
' but it must be with our hands, not with our Brutus'
feet.' Then taking every man by the hand, he saying of flying with
said these words unto them with a cheerful hands & not with
*countenance. ' It rejoiceth my heart that not feet.
*one of my friends hath failed me at my need, and I do not
*complain of my fortune, but only for my country's sake :
*for, as for me, I think myself happier than they that have
*overcome, considering that I leave a perpetual fame of our
*courage and manhood, the which our enemies the conquer-

[1] Cf Julius Caesar, V. v. 2, 3.   [2] Ibid. V. v. 5-12.
" Ibid. V. v. 25-29.   [4] Ibid. V. v. 30.

ors shall never attain unto by force nor money, neither can*
let their posterity to say that they, being naughty and*
unjust men, have slain good men, to usurp tyrannical*
power not pertaining to them.'[1] Having said so, he*
prayed every man to shift for themselves, and then he went
a little aside with two or three only, among the which
Strato was one, with whom he came first acquainted
by the study of Rhetoric. He came as near to
him as he could, and taking his sword by the hilts
with both his hands, and falling down upon the
point of it, ran himself through. Others say that,*
not he, but Strato (at his request) held the sword in his*
hand, and turned his head aside, and that Brutus fell down*
upon it : and so ran himself through, and died presently.[2]*
Messala, that had been Brutus' great friend, became afterwards Octavius Caesar's friend. So, shortly after,
Caesar being at good leisure, he brought Strato
Brutus' friend unto him, and weeping, said :
'Caesar, behold, here is he that did the last†
service to my Brutus.'[3] Caesar welcomed him at that time,†
and afterwards he did him as faithful service in all his affairs,
as any Grecian else he had about him, until the
battle of Actium. It is reported also, that this
Messala himself answered Caesar one day, when
he gave him great praise before his face, that he had

Brutus slew himself.

Strato, Brutus' familiar and friend.

Strato received into Caesar's friendship.

Messala Corvinus, Brutus' friend.

---

[1] Cf. *Julius Caesar*, V. v. 33-8.   [2] *Ibid.* V. v. 47-51.
[3] *Ibid.* V. v. 66, 7.

MARCUS BRUTUS

fought valiantly, and with great affection for him, at the battle of Actium, (notwithstanding that he had been his cruel enemy before, at the battle of Philippi, for Brutus' sake) · 'I ever loved,' said he, 'to take the best and justest part' Now, Antonius having found Brutus' body, he caused it to be wrapped up in one of the richest coat armours he had. Afterwards also, Antonius understanding that this coat armour was stolen, he put the thief to death that had stolen it, and sent the ashes of his body unto Servilia his mother. And for Porcia, Brutus' wife, Nicolaus the Philosopher and *Valerius Maximus do write, that she determining *to kill herself (her parents and friends carefully *looking to her to keep her from it) took hot burn-*ing coals, and cast them into her mouth, and kept *her mouth so close that she choked herself.[1] There was a letter of Brutus found written to his friends, complaining of their negligence, that his wife being sick, they would not help her, but suffered her to kill herself, choosing to die, rather than to languish in pain. Thus it appeareth that Nicolaus knew not well that time, sith the letter (at the least if it were Brutus' letter) doth plainly declare the disease and love of this Lady, and also the manner of her death.

margin: Brutus' funerals

margin: Porcia, Brutus' wife, killed herself with burning coals.

[1] Cf. *Julius Caesar*, IV. iii. 151–6.

NOTES

THE LIFE OF JULIUS CAESAR

P. 3, ll. 9, 11. *Miletus.* The old editions have *Miletum,* an erroneous expansion of Amyot's *Milet.* North seems never to have had recourse in case of difficulty to a Latin or Greek text of Plutarch. Practically all his mistranslations are due to his effort to follow Amyot where the latter's language is ambiguous or obscure. In almost every instance reference to the Greek version would have set him right at once. It is especially noteworthy that in the names of persons and places he either takes over the Gallicized form directly or else Anglicizes it, as here, purely by guess.

P. 5, l. 14. *quail.* The word here retains its original signification, 'to die, perish,' as in O.E. *cwelan.*

P. 6, l. 5. *scratch.* This is the form found in the text of 1595 and subsequent editions. The 1579 folio reads *scrat.*

P. 7, l. 19. *bought good cheap.* 'Cheap' is, of course, here a noun, as in 'Cheapside,' and has the meaning of 'bargain.' The phrase 'good cheap' is really prepositional, a word like 'at' being understood before it, but it occurs in just the present use at least as early as the M.E. *Ayenbite of Inwit.*

l. 23. *highway going unto Appius.* Such is the reading of the first two editions, a stupid mistranslation of Amyot's 'chemin qui s'appelle la uoye d'Appius.' The edition of 1603 gives the obvious correction, 'the highway called Appius way.'

P. 8, ll. 12, 13. *in their greatest ruff.* The French has, 'en leur plus grande uogue.' The word 'ruff' in this sense is common in Elizabethan usage; cf. *Sir Thomas More*, II. iv. 99, 'And you in ruff of your opynions clothd.'

l. 14. *of victories that carried triumphs*: 'des uictoires qui portoient des trophees.' The Greek has Νίκας τροπαιοφόρους.

P. 9, ll. 20, 21. *that hardily he should give place to no man*: 'qu'il prist hardiment cueur de ne ceder à personne.'

l. 24. *chief Bishop.* This is a rather startling anachronism in which North persists. Amyot has quite regularly 'le souuerain Pontife.' The office is, of course, that of Pontifex Maximus, to which Caesar was elected in the year 63 B.C.

P. 10, l. 7. *lend* should be 'borrow.' Amyot's word is 'emprunteroit.' Plutarch wrote προσδανεισάμενος.

P. 11, l. 16. *best appear.* So edd. 1579, 1595. The editions of 1603 and after read 'appear best.'

P. 13, l. 19. *nymph of wood*: 'dryad,' νύμφην Δρυάδα.

P. 15, l. 15. *slanaered.* The proper meaning of the word appears from Amyot's reading, 'à qui il auoit faict cest oultrage.' Cf., for another instance, the *Life of Brutus*, p. 112, l. 24.

P. 17, l. 22. *Calaïcans.* The old editions of North spell 'Callæcians,' following Amyot's 'Callæciens.' Plutarch writes Καλλαικούς.

l. 23. *Oceanus.* Old editions, 'Oceanum'; again an error due to the attempt to Latinize the French 'Oceane.'

P. 20, l. 9. *let* : 'hinder.'

l. 21. *made sure* : 'betrothed.'

ll. 22, 23. *Pompey's daughter.* This is the correction of ed. 1603. The first two editions have 'Pompey's wife,' a mistake caused by the ambiguity of Amyot's 'celle de Pompeius.'

P. 21, l. 15. *Gaul on this side* : 'Cisalpine Gaul.' The edition of 1579 gives 'Gaul on his side,' corrected in ed 1595. Amyot reads 'toutes les Gaules, tant de deça que de dela les monts.'

P. 22, l. 1. *that would be President of the Senate under him* : a complete mistranslation. Plutarch wrote: Τῶν δὲ ἄλλων συγκλητικῶν ὀλίγοι παντάπασιν αὐτῷ συνῄεσαν. Amyot translates : 'il y eut peu des Senateurs qui se uoulussent trouuer soubz luy President au Senat,' where 'President' is, of course, to be construed with 'luy.'

P. 26, ll. 14, 15. *thereby bestowed his rest, to make him always able to do something* : 'employant par ce moien son repos à faire tousiours quelque chose.'

P. 28, l. 8. *Arar.* Both in the text and in the marginal note the old editions of North read 'Arax,' though Amyot gives the proper form 'Arar.'

l. 20. *distress their camp* : 'take their camp.' Cf. *N.E.D.*, s.v. *Distress*, v., 2.

l. 21 *strength* : 'rempart' in Amyot.

P. 31, l. 7. *Sequanes :* 'Sequaniens' in Amyot.

P. 32, l. 8. *the Nervians.* The form of the proper name here agrees as usual with the French, 'Nerviens.' In the marginal note, however, we find the Latin form, 'Nervii.'

*

There are no marginal notes in Amyot except a very few dealing principally with textual criticism. From various discrepancies between the notes in North and the text, it would seem probable that the former were not written by the translator, but were later inserted by the publisher for the comfort of readers. Cf. my notes to the *Life of Coriolanus*, Vol. II. pp. 152, 202, and to p. 103, l. 10 of this volume.

l. 13. *six-score thousand fighting men*. Plutarch's number, 60,000, has been exactly doubled; but cf. p. 33, l. 2, where we have the proper computation, 'three-score thousand.' Such irregularities in reckoning are the rule rather than the exception in Amyot and North; they are really of no consequence, and indicate merely the ease with which mistakes in numerals crept into all ancient texts.

P. 33, l. 23. *Luca*. Here the old editions have *Luke*, corresponding to Amyot's 'Lucques,' whereas the marginal note gives *Luca*.

P. 34, l. 14. *Favonius*. 'Faonius' old editions and Amyot, corresponding to the Greek Φαώνιος. I follow modern editors in using the Latin form.

l. 26. *Ipes*. The proper form would be 'Usipes.' The mistake is due to a corruption in the Greek text of Plutarch by which Οὐσίπας became οὖς Ἴπας.

P. 37, ll. 2–7. *to make war in that so great and famous Island . . . inhabitable*. North's national pride is here responsible for the addition of an adjective or two and for the slurring over of the reference to the conquest of Britain. The corresponding passage in Amyot runs as follows: 'pour aller faire la guerre en ceste isle, si grande, que plusieurs des anciens n'ont pas uoulu croire qu'elle fust en nature, & qui a mis plusieurs historiens en grande dispute, maintenans que c'estoit chose faulse & controuuee à plaisir, & luy fut le premier qui commencea à la conquerir.'

l. 22. *tickle* : 'insecure.' Cf. p. 181, l. 6.

P. 38, ll. 22, 23. *making accompt that he was but a handful in their hands, they were so few.* The pronouns are decidedly mixed ; Amyot's version is much clearer : 'faisans leur compte, qu'ilz l'éporteroient tout du premier coup, à cause qu'il auoit si peu de gens.'

P. 40, l. 12. *towards the sea Adriatic.* The marginal note to these words is one of Amyot's, where it runs, 'Les autres lisent en ce lieu, πρὸς τὸν Ἄραριν, qui seroit à dire iusqu'à la riuiere de la Sone.' The alternative reading is the one which all modern editors of Plutarch have adopted.

l. 19. *very valiant.* The editions of 1595, etc., omit 'very.'

l. 25. *unvincible.* Edd. 1603, etc., change to 'invincible.'

P. 41, l. 6. *Aedui.* Old editions have 'Hedui' = Amyot's 'Heduiens.

P. 43, ll. 26, 27. *who only did see that one of them two must needs fall.* This is vilely translated from Amyot and fails entirely to convey Plutarch's idea in ὃς ἦν ἔφεδρος ἀμφοῖν. The French is, 'qui seul pouuoit espier que l'un d'eulx deux donnast en terre,' which means that Crassus was the only Roman sufficiently powerful to look on till one of the competitors should be overcome, and then join combat with the survivor.

P. 44, ll. 2-4. *neither did anything let Pompey to withstand that it should not come to pass.* Clumsily and probably incorrectly translated. Amyot reads, 'ny à Pompeius pour obuier à ce que cela ne luy aduinst,' where *cela* refers to becoming the greatest person at Rome. The Greek is somewhat different: ἀπελέιπετο τῷ μὲν (Caesar) ὑπὲρ τοῦ γενέσθαι μεγίστῳ τον ὄντα (Pompey) καταλύειν, τῷ δὲ (Pompey), ἵνα μὴ πάθῃ τοῦτο, προαναιρεῖν ὅν ἐδεδοίκει.

P. 49, 1. 6. *Marcellus.* So Amyot, by mistake, but Plutarch says 'Lentulus.'

P. 50, ll. 20, 21. *a great city of Gaul, being the first city men come to, when they come out of Gaul*: 'grande uille, que l'on rencontre la premiere au sortir de la Gaule.'

P. 52, l. 4. *A desperate man feareth no danger*: 'A tout perdre n'y a qu'un coup perilleux.' The marginal note to this passage is translated from Amyot.

P. 54, l. 4. *garboil*: 'commotion.' Cf. *Life of Brutus*, p. 113, l. 6.

P. 55, l. 2. *carriage*: 'tout son bagage.' North uses the word repeatedly in this sense. Cf. p. 177, l. 17; Vol. II. p. 59, l. 26.

P. 64, ll. 25, 26. *so many captains.* So the edition of 1579; the later editions all read 'many captains,' but wrongly, for the French is 'tant de Capitaines.'

P. 65, l. 17. *Gomphi in Thessaly.* The old editions of North follow the spelling of Amyot both here and in the margin, reading 'Gomphes.'

l. 23. *Baccherians.* Amyot has 'Bacchanales,' Plutarch 'Βακχεύοντες.'

P. 66, l. 5. *hands.* This passage is obviously incoherent. Amyot gives the following note, disregarded by North: 'L'original Grec est defectueux en cest ēdroit, & le faut rēplir de ce qui est cy deuāt escrit en la uie de Pompeius, feuillet 458 soubs la lettre C.' The passage in question runs: 'Et la nuict ensuiuant il fut aduis à Pompeius en

NOTES

dormant, qu'il entroit dedans le Theatre, là ou le peuple le recueilloit auec grands battemens de mains par honneur, & que luy ornoit le temple de Venus uictorieuse de plusieurs despouilles. Ceste uision de songe d'un costé luy donnoit bon courage, & d'un autre costé le luy rompoit aussi, pour autant qu'il auoit peur, qu'estant la race de Caesar descendue de la deesse Venus, son songe ne uoulust signifier qu'elle seroit annoblie & illustree par la uictoire & par les despouilles qu'il gagneroit sur luy.' Modern editors of Plutarch bracket the Greek sentence corresponding to 'For he thought—hands' as spurious.

ll. 8, 9. *the chief Bishopric* : 'le souuerain Pōtificat.' Cf. note to p. 9, l. 24.

P. 67, l. 13. *dost thou think* : a mistaken translation ot Amyot's imperative, 'attens toy.'

l. 17. *the element* : that is, par excellence, the element of air. Cf. *N.E.D.*, s.v. *Element*, sb. 10.

P. 69, l. 9. *a box on the ear.* Quite wrong. Amyot's word 'soufflet' has here the sense of 'bellows.' Cf. Littré's dictionary, s v. 1⁰. The simile is not in the Greek.

P. 70, l. 9. *but to seek . . . and to hurt.* Instances of the so-called absolute infinitive construction. Cf. Kellner, *Historical Outlines of English Syntax*, §§ 399, 400.

P. 72, l. 23. *give.* So the second and later editions of North. The *editio princeps* reads 'gaue,' but Amyot's phrase is 'se commence.'

P. 73, l. 14. *at o' side.* Edd. 1579, 1595 read 'at toe side,' which is merely a Middle English form of the words in the text. The preposition and article have been merged, as in Chaucer's 'atten ale,' 'atte beste,' and in redividing the final consonant of 'at' has remained with the article ; cf. 'the tother' < 'that other.' *o*' is a weakened form of 'one' (ān), which originally might serve either as indefinite article or as numeral. The edition of 1603, not understanding the idiom 'at toe side,' substituted 'aside'; modern editors have printed 'at one side.'

P. 74, l. 17. *treen*: 'wooden.' O.E. 'trēowen,' the adjective belonging to *trēo*, 'tree.'

P. 76, l. 19. *holding divers books in his hand*: 'tenant plusieurs papiers en l'une de ses mains.' It is very likely that this passage suggested to Shakespeare the episode of Caesar's swimming match with Cassius (*Julius Caesar*, I. ii. 100-115). Cf. also the last speech but one of Achillas in *The False One* (V. iv.).

P. 79, l. 11. *battles he fought*: 'battles fought,' 1595, etc.

l. 13. *Sallution*. So Amyot; the old editions of North give wrongly, 'Sallutius.'

P. 81, l. 13. *Praetors and Consuls*: 'Praetor and Consuls,' 1595, etc. Amyot's phrase is 'personnages de dignité Praetoriale ou Consulaire.'

P. 82, l. 9. *for a civil*: 'for civil,' 1595, etc.

l. 21. *allowing*: 'commending,' the common M.E. sense. Cf. also p. 104, l. 1.

P. 88, l. 11. *Persians*. Plutarch and Amyot have 'Parthians,' which is right, but cf. note to Vol. II. p. 57, l. 12.

l. 24. *Circeii*. 'Circees' in old editions and Amyot.

P. 89, l. 1. *seaw*: 'drain.' Amyot writes, 'de destourner l'eau.'

P. 91, l. 21. *standing of their feet*: 'standing on their feet,' ed. 1595, etc. The use of the preposition *of*, or its

NOTES

abbreviation *o'*, in such cases is almost too common to call for notice. Cf. Vol. II. p. 17, l. 10.

P. 93, l. 13. *with Diadems upon their heads.* In Shakespeare it is only scarfs which Flavius and Marullus pull off. Cf. *Julius Caesar*, I. ii. 290.

l. 18. *Brutes.* We should expect 'Bruti' or 'Brutuses,' but North keeps the Gallicized form of Amyot.

P. 94, l. 10. *many more of his friends besides.* Instead of 'more' the 1595 edition gives the old adverbial form 'moe.'

P. 95, l. 23. *the solitary birds.* So ed. 1595, etc.; the folio of 1579 gives 'these solitary birds,' but Amyot's rendering is 'des oyseaux solitaires.'

P. 96, l. 17 *to the Soothsayer.* For 'to' ed. 1595, etc., read 'vnto.'

P. 97, l. 25. *none did like them* : 'ne luy en promettoient rien de bon.' For *like* in the common Elizabethan sense of 'please,' cf. *N.E.D.*, s.v. *Like*, v¹, 1.

P. 98, l. 2. *Decius Brutus.* Amyot reads 'Decimus,' which is Plutarch's word.

l. 25. *to dismiss them.* Another instance of the 'absolute infinitive.' Cf. note to p. 70, l 9.

P. 99, l. 5. *unto his house.* The edition of 1595 replaces 'unto' by 'into.'

P. 100, l. 15. *beside.* 'besides' in the old editions.

l. 18. *Decius Brutus Albinus.* In the *Life of Brutus*, p. 132, l. 8, as in Shakespeare, it is Trebonius who decoys Antony away. Perhaps these lines ought not to be marked with asterisks, as Shakespeare's plain debt is rather to the version of the same incident in the *Life of Brutus.* Probably, though, both accounts were in the poet's mind.

NOTES

l. 24. *Metellus Cimber.* The name should be 'Tullius Cimber,' as in Plutarch and in North's version of the *Life of Brutus*; cf. p. 132, l. 15. The mistake is due to Amyot. Here Shakespeare follows the *Life of Caesar* rather than that of Brutus.

P. 101, ll. 19, 20. *that they had no power to fly.* The folio of 1595 and its successors omit 'that.'

P. 102, l. 11. *gore-blood.* A common intensive with North; cf. *Life of Brutus*, p. 126, ll. 17, 18.

l. 16. *three and twenty wounds.* Shakespeare says 'three and thirty,' possibly a mere slip of the memory.

P. 103, l. 10, marginal note. *do go to the market-place.* Instead of 'market-place' the editions of 1579, 1595 read 'Capitoll,' which the later folios altered to make the note agree with the text (l. 9). Cf. note to p. 32, l. 8.

l. 16. *among.* Folio 1595, etc., read 'amongest.'

P. 104, l. 19. *their houses that had slain Caesar.* 'their' has here retained its original character of personal pronoun in the genitive; it is the antecedent of the relative.

P. 105, l. 10. *one of mean sort*: 'one of the mean sort' ed. 1595, etc.

ll. 24, 25. *and Pompey also lived not passing four years more than he.* This is not by any means the significance of the French, '& ne suruescut Pompeius gueres plus de quattre ans.' North has taken the object of the verb for its subject, led astray no doubt by the preservation of the Latin nominative termination. The Greek is perfectly clear: Πομπηίῳ δ' ἐπιβιώσας οὐ πολὺ πλέον ἐτῶν τεσσάρων.

P. 106, ll. 12, 13. *at the journey of Philippi.* For 'journey' in sense of 'battle' cf. *N.E.D.* s.v. 7. North follows Amyot's 'apres auoir esté desfait en bataille en la iournée de

NOTES

Philippes.' It should be added that both here and elsewhere the old editions of North retain the French form of the proper name, *Philippes*.

l. 17. *the eight night.* 'Eight' is here a weakened form of the ordinal 'eighth,' as often in early English. Cf. *N.E.D.* s.v. *Eighth.*

l. 24. *rotted before it could ripe.* The use of 'ripe' in this way illustrates one of the most striking features of the Elizabethan language, the facility with which verbs could be made out of adjectives, nouns or any other part of speech.

P. 108, ll. 4-6. For a more detailed account of the death of Brutus, cf. pp. 189, 190.

THE LIFE OF MARCUS BRUTUS

P. 109, l. 12. *presently* : 'at present.'

P. 110, l. 3. *Ahala.* The word is spelled 'Hala' in Amyot and the early editions of North.

l. 10. *Servilius.* So, correctly, the editions of 1579, 1603, etc. The folio of 1595 gives 'Brutus' by mistake. Amyot uses the pronoun 'il,' referring obviously to Servilius.

P. 111, ll. 2, 3. *whom Brutus studied most to follow of all the other Romans.* An illogical idiom exceedingly popular with Elizabethan writers.

l. 19. *He* : *i.e.* Brutus.

P. 112, l. 23. *Canidius.* 'Caninius' in Amyot and early editions of North, with marginal note, 'Ou Canidius,' 'Or Canidius.'

P. 113, l. 8. *unto death* : 'to death' 1595, etc.

l. 9. *respect of*: 'consideration for.' Cf. *N.E.D.*, s.v. *Respect*, sb. 13.

P. 114, ll. 2–4. *marginal note*. Omitted 1595, etc.

ll. 2, 3. *not only the days before, but the self same day also before the great battle*. Translated over literally from Amyot's 'non seulement tous les iours precedẽts, mais aussi celuy mesme de deuant la grande battaille.'

P. 115, l. 8. *a love letter* : 'une lettre amatoire & lascifue.'

l. 10. *drunken sop* : 'yurogne.'

P. 116, *marginal note*. This is one of Amyot's notes, merely translated by North; the French reads: 'C'estoit Iuba, mais il est certaĩ que Brutus interceda aussi pour Deiotarus, Roy de Galatie, qui neãtmoins fut par Cęsar priué d'une grãde partie de son païs. Et pource seroit plus à propos entendre ce lieu de luy.'

P. 118, ll. 6, 7. *objections* : 'representations.' Cf. *N.E.D.*, s.v. 4.

P. 119, l. 8. *think ye that Brutus will not tarry till this body die*. This is the proper rendering; cf. *Life of Caesar*, p. 94, ll. 21, 22, where the wording is, 'Brutus will look for this skin.' The Greek has Τί δέ; οὐκ ἂν ὑμῖν δοκεῖ Βροῦτος ἀναμεῖναι τουτὶ τὸ σαρκίον;

l. 13. *to have been next unto Caesar*. So folio 1595, etc.; instead of 'to' folio 1579 reads 'and', which is possible, but not so smooth or so near the French, 's'il eust peu endurer de seconder Caesar quelque espace de temps.'

ll. 18, 19. *could evil away with* : 'portoit mal patiemment.'

P. 120, ll. 8, 9. *But this holdeth no water* : 'mais ilz ne disent pas la verité.'

ll. 14, 15. *two good whirts on the ear* . 'une couple de soufflets.'

ll. 21, 22. *that my fists may walk once again about thine ears.* This is a not infrequent Elizabethan use of the word 'walk'; cf. *Thomas Lord Cromwell*, I. ii. 29, 'No hammers walking and my worke to do.'

P. 121, ll. 12, 13. *as we have written more at large in Julius Caesar's life* : viz. p. 93.

l. 18. *it stood them upon* : 'it concerned them.'

l. 20. *by his only presence.* We should say, 'by the presence of him alone.'

P. 122, l. 2. *grew strange together* : 'became estranged'

l. 15. *to die for the liberty* : a Gallicism. Amyot has regularly enough 'la liberté.' The editor of the folio of 1603 attempted to improve matters by substituting 'thy' for 'the,' which, however, does not give the sense.

P. 123, ll. 5–8, *marginal note.* One of Amyot's glosses.

l. 18. *acquaintance* : 'acquitance,' folio 1595. A mere misprint.

P. 124, ll. 1–6. Cicero is omitted from the conspiracy in Shakespeare's play, not because of his cowardice, as here, but

'For he will never follow anything
That other men begin' (II. i. 151, 152).

l. 10. *Favonius.* The word is regularly spelled 'Faonius' in Amyot and the old editions of North. Cf. note to p. 34, l. 14 above.

ll. 14, 15. *for a sight of ignorant fools and asses* : 'pour des folz & des ignorans.'

P. 125, l. 5. *the only name* : 'the name alone.'

P. 126, l. 10. *well seen in* : 'well informed about.' Cf. *Dr. Faustus*, l. 168, 'Inricht with tongues, well seene in minerals.'

P. 129, l. 27. *Laena*. The correct Greek form is Λαίνας, but Shakespeare agrees with Amyot and North in adopting the Latinized spelling.

P. 130, l. 2. *rounded* : 'whispered,' from M.E. 'rounen.' The 'd' is parasitic, as in 'sound.'

P. 131, ll. 16, 17. *it was no tarrying for them till they were apprehended*. An Elizabethan equivalent of Amyot's 'qu'il ne falloit pas attendre iusques à ce que lon les saisist au corps.' The Greek has ὡς χρὴ μὴ περιμένειν σύλληψιν, which is rendered in Latin, 'non esse exspectandum donec caperentur.'

l. 23. *companion*. Amyot has 'cõpagnons,' which answers to Plutarch's τοὺς περὶ Κάσσιον. North's reading may be a misprint, or it may refer like the Latin version to Cassius alone, 'nam . . . verbis uti non licebat, Cassium confirmavit.' 'Cassius,' in l. 26, ought strictly to be 'Cassius and his companions' (τοὺς περὶ Κάσσιον ἐθάρρυνε).

P. 132, l. 9. *at o' side*. Ed. 1579 prints in one word, 'atoside.' Cf. note to p. 73, l. 14. The editions of 1595 ff. have 'aside.'

P. 133, l. 6. *on a heap*: a relic of the common Old English use in adverbial phrases. Cf. 'among,' 'a-fishing' (O.E. on gemonge, on fiscunge).

l. 20. *fact*. The word is commonly used by Elizabethan writers in the sense of 'deed,' and generally, as here, with an unfavourable connotation.

ll. 24, 25. *to look to defend their liberty* : 'à tascher de recouurer la liberté.'

l. 27. *a wicked man, and that in nature favoured tyranny*. A Gallicism. Amyot writes, 'un homme insolēt, & qui de sa nature fauorisoit à la monarchie.'

P. 137, l. 1. *in hugger mugger* : 'in careless haste.' The phrase is a very common piece of Elizabethan slang. Cf. *N.E.D.* for instances.

P. 138, l. 10. *midst*. The folio of 1579 regularly spells the word 'middest.'

P. 141, l. 24-27. *and, for his own part, that he had never resolutely determined with himself to make war, or peace, but otherwise, that he was certainly minded never to be slave nor subject.* The English is not quite clear, but there is no ambiguity about the French reading : 'Et que de sa part il n'auoit iamais resoluement arresté en soymesme de faire ny la paix, ny la guerre, mais que sa resolution & sa deliberation arrestee estoit de iamais ne seruir.'

P. 142, l. 8. *other*. The proper pronominal form of the plural, corresponding to O.E. ōðre. In North's time usage was fluctuating, and in the second edition (1595) of the Lives the form 'others,' after the analogy of plural nouns, has become the usual one.

l. 9. *making portsale of their service* : 'uendans leur seruice, ne plus ne moins qu'à un encan.'

l. 12. *Luke*. Amyot, following the Greek, gives 'Lucanie.'

P. 143, l. 4. *all in all*. So ed. 1595 ff. The folio of 1579 omits the first 'all.' North's translations from Homer are very free. Amyot reads in the present case :

'Hector, tu tiens lieu de pere & de mere
En mon endroit, de mary & de frere.'

l. 8, 9. Amyot's translation of these lines runs :

'Il ne te fault d'autre chose mesler,
Que d'enseigner tes femmes à filer.'

l. 15. *embarking at Elea in Luke*.   Amyot has simply 'An partir de là,' translating the Greek Ἀναχθεὶς δ' ὁ Βροῦτος ἐκεῖθεν.

P. 144, ll. 22, 23.   Amyot reads:

> 'Mais toutefois ma triste destinee
> Et Phœbus ont ma uie terminee.'

P. 145, l. 10. *forged*.   The folio 1595 has the misprint 'forced,' retained by one of the modern editors.   The French word is 'forgees.'

l. 21. *snew*.   An old preterite.

P. 146, l. 26. *Buthrotum*.   'Buthrotus' in Amyot and North.

P. 147, l. 12. *without stroke striking* : 'sans coup ferir.'

P. 149, l. 12. *two hundred of the noblest men of Rome*. There is great inconsistency as to the number. Compare the corresponding passages in *Julius Caesar* (IV. iii. 174–6) and in the *Life of Antonius*, Vol. II. p. 29.

P. 150, l. 9. *Cyzicus* : 'Cyzicum' Amyot and North.

l. 27. *Piraeus*.   Amyot gives 'Piræe,' which North wrongly Anglicizes 'Piræa.'

P. 151, l. 4. *departing*.   So the first edition, rightly ; the second folio changes to 'departed.' Amyot's reading is, 'estans partiz,' translating the Greek Ὁρμήσαντες.

ll. 20, 21. *well-beloved of the people and his own* : 'biē uoulu du peuple, aimé des siēs.'

P. 155, l. 18. *of a fire :* 'on fire' ed. 1595 ff.

P. 156, l. 19. *with their own hands*.   The first edition omits 'with.'

P. 158, l. 24. *sufficienter*.   Ed. 1595 ff. read 'sufficient,' but the comparative is certainly right.   Amyot has 'plus suffisans' and the Greek phrase is δι' ἐρημίαν ἀνδρῶν βελτιόνων.

P. 159, l. 24. *called them both Emperors.* Amyot has the following note : 'Imperatores, c'est à dire souuerains Capitaines.'

P. 161, ll 5, 6. North takes great liberties with Homer's Ἀλλὰ πίθεσθ'. ἄμφω δὲ νεωτέρω ἐστὸν ἐμεῖο Amyot's rendering is much closer :

> 'Escoutez moy, & mon conseil suyuez :
> I'ay plus uescu, que tous deux uous n'auez'

l. 24—p. 162, l. 3. North's English is here rather obscure. Amyot's rendering runs : 'à cause que peu de iours au parauāt, luy mesme auoit seulement admonesté de paroles en priué deux de ses amis attaincts & conuaincus de mesmes crimes, & en public les auoit absouls, & ne laissoit pas de les employer & de s'en seruir comme deuant.'

P. 163, l. 9. *Captains, petty Captains, and Colonels*: 'Capitaines, Cēteniers & Chefz de bēdes.' The Greek has ἑκατοντάρχαι και χιλίαρχοι.

l. 15. *that he saw.* Amyot has simply 'aperceut.'

P. 165. ll. 24, 25. *had not Antonius' aid been*: 'had it not been for, etc.,' a common construction. 'Aid' is probably used in sense of Latin *auxilia*, 'troops.' Amyot's wording is very similar : 'n'eust esté le secours d'Antonius.'

P. 166, ll. 18, 19. *and be afraid.* So ed. 1579 ; the second and later editions read wrongly 'and to be afraid,' which does not answer to the French '& craignent.'

P. 167, l. 5. *day of the battle.* 'day of battle' ed. 1595 ff.

l. 12. *at another time.* 'at' is omitted in ed. 1595 ff.

P. 168, l. 22. *If I get nought else.* Ed. 1595 ff. replace 'nought' by 'nothing.'

P. 169, ll. 21, 22. *the signal of battle . . . which was an arming scarlet coat* : σύμβολον ἀγῶνος φοινικοῦς χιτὼν. For 'arming' in the sense of 'that calls to arms,' cf. N.E.D., s.v.

P. 170, l. 8. *I trust.* The present of continued action. We should say 'I trusted.' North varies from Amyot and Plutarch considerably in this passage. The Greek reads οὐκ οἶδ' ὅπως ἐν φιλοσοφίᾳ λόγον ἀφῆκα μέγαν, which Amyot renders, rather incorrectly, 'ie feis, ne sçay comment, un discours de Philosophie.'

P. 177, l. 17. *carriage* : 'baggage'; cf. note to p. 55, l. 2.

P. 178, ll. 22, 23. *them that were overcome—those that did overcome.* The antithesis is better brought out in the first edition of North, where the first 'overcome' is spelled, after the manner of strong past participles, 'ouercomen.'

P. 181, l. 6. *tickle* : cf. note to p. 37, l. 22.

P. 182, ll. 15, 16. *distressed* : cf. note to p. 28, l. 20.

P. 183, l. 12. *doth make no mention of this spirit.* 'no' is omitted in the edition of 1579, an obvious printer's error corrected in ed. 1595. Amyot says, 'ne fait point de mêtion de ce fantasme,' and the Greek also has the negative, οὐ λέγει.

P. 184, l. 14. *a-horseback* : 'on horseback' 1595 ff.

P. 188, ll. 1, 2. Amyot's version of the Greek verse is:

> 'O Iupiter, que celuy, dont naissance
> Ont tant de maulx, n'eschappe ta uengeance.'

The marginal note here comes from Amyot, 'Appiā l'ētend d'Antonius.'

l. 8. *pioneers*: soldiers employed in tasks of engineering. Cf. *N.E.D.*, s.v. 1.

l. 9, 10. *he ran to the river for water, and brought it in his sallet.* Amyot says simply, 's'en courut auec un cabasset uers la riuière.' 'Sallet' is a species of helmet.

l. 19. *Furthermore.* This is not a good rendering of Plutarch's particle, δὲ. 'Hence' or 'however' would be better. Amyot has 'Au reste' and the Latin translation 'Inde.'

P. 190, l. 2. *naughty.* In North's time the word was, of course, employed in a much more serious sense than at present. Cf. *N.E.D.*, s.v. 2.

P. 191, l. 21. *knew not well that time.* There is no reason for the use of the demonstrative 'that.' Amyot says, 'n'auroit pas bië cogneu le temps,' and the Latin version renders ἠγνοηκέναι τὸν χρόνον correctly by 'ignorasse mortis tempus.'

BIBLIOLIFE

Old Books Deserve a New Life
www.bibliolife.com

Did you know that you can get most of our titles in our trademark **EasyScript**[TM] print format? **EasyScript**[TM] provides readers with a larger than average typeface, for a reading experience that's easier on the eyes.

Did you know that we have an ever-growing collection of books in many languages?

Order online:
www.bibliolife.com/store

Or to exclusively browse our **EasyScript**[TM] collection:
www.bibliogrande.com

At BiblioLife, we aim to make knowledge more accessible by making thousands of titles available to you – quickly and affordably.

Contact us:
BiblioLife
PO Box 21206
Charleston, SC 29413

CPSIA information can be obtained at www.ICGtesting.com
Printed in the USA
BVOW05s1424190214

345417BV00025B/603/P